Author's Acknowledgement
A special thank you to my husband Denys for the patience,
understanding and wholehearted support which, as ever, he gave to me
during the writing and compilation of this book.

This edition published in 1993 by SMITHMARK Publishers, Inc.,
16 East 32nd Street, New York, NY 10016.

SMITHMARK books are available for bulk purchase for sales promotion
and premium use. For details write or call the manager of special sales,
SMITHMARK Publishers Inc., 16 East 32nd Street,
New York, NY 10016; (212) 532-6600.

3137
Produced by CLB Publishing Ltd
Godalming Business Centre
Woolsack Way
Godalming, Surrey GU7 1XW

ISBN 0 8317 5169 X

Managing Editor: Jo Finnis

Editor: William Harris

Design: Paul Tanner and Sue Pressley

Captions: Louise Houghton

Typesetting: Julie Smith

Photographs: Cogis Agency – Annette Amblin; Bernard Bernic;
Philippe Garguil; Jean-Claude Gissey; Jean-Michel Labat; Gérard Lacz;
Yves Lanceau; Sylvie Lepage; François Nicaise; Hervé Nicolle;
Gérald Potier; François Varin; Serge Vedic; Frank Vidal; Paola Visintini

Illustrations: Pam Martins; Terry Burton courtesy Bernard Thornton
Artists, London (astrological portraits)

Production: Ruth Arthur; Sally Connolly; Neil Randles

Director of Production: Gerald Hughes

Printed in Spain by Graficromo, S.A.

10 9 8 7 6 5 4 3 2 1

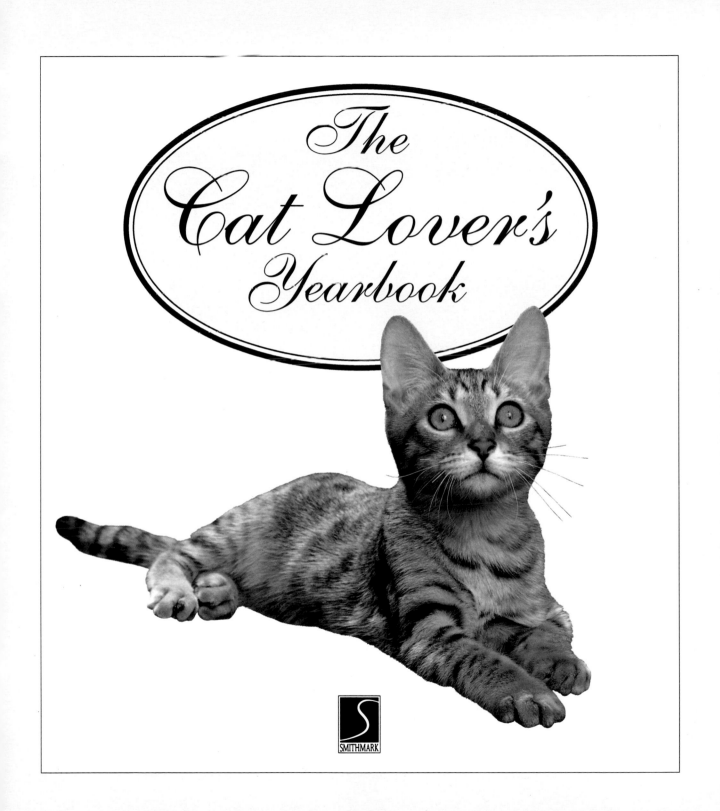

The Cat Lover's Yearbook

SMITHMARK

~ *Introduction* ~

The Cat Lover's Yearbook is for all those who have known and have loved the cat. An intriguing treasury of fascinating feline fact and fable, recounting details of historical cats; heroic cats; famous people and their cats; cat breeds whose myth and origin reach back into the mists of time; superstitions; little-known legends about the cat and a keenly observed astrological section enabling the cat lover to better understand the vagaries of pussy's behavior! This unique book is also a delightful way in which to "cat"-alogue the birthdays of family, friends and felines, anniversaries and special days to remember.

Exquisitely presented and illustrated throughout, *The Cat Lover's Yearbook* will be a joy to give or to receive and certainly to cherish, forever ...

The "Sacred Cat of Burma," the Birman is distinguished by four white gloves.

~ *January* ~

"Refined and delicate natures understand the cat. Women, poets, and artists hold it in great esteem, for they recognize the exquisite delicacy of its nervous system; indeed, only coarse natures fail to discern the natural distinction of the cat."

Les Chats, Champfleury, 1885

The intuitive January cat can be a loyal and trustworthy companion.

~ 1 ~

~ 2 ~

SUPERSTITIOUS CATS
A cat is very often kept as a lucky mascot in the theater and disaster strikes any actor who dares to kick it.

~ 3 ~

~ 4 ~

~ 5 ~

CATS WITH CONNECTIONS
White Heather belonged to England's Queen Victoria (1819-1901). Reminding the Queen of her beloved Scotland, White Heather lived at Buckingham Palace and on surviving Victoria's death was "adopted" by her successor, King Edward VII.

~ 6 ~

~ 7 ~

CAT SNIPS
When Theodore Roosevelt was President of the United States, there were several cats in the White House, including Tom Quartz, a kitten belonging to the president's son, Kermit. In one of his letters to the boy, the president reported; "… the next Speaker of the House, Mr. Cannon, an exceedingly solemn elderly gentleman with chin whiskers, who certainly does not look to be of a playful nature, came to call upon me. …Tom Quartz strolled by, his tail erect and very fluffy. He spied Mr. Cannon going down the stairs, jumped to the conclusion that he was a playmate escaping, and raced after him, suddenly grasping him by the leg … then loosening his hold, he tore downstairs ahead of Mr. Cannon, who eyed him with an iron calm and not one particle of surprise."

The American Shorthair, a handsome breed.

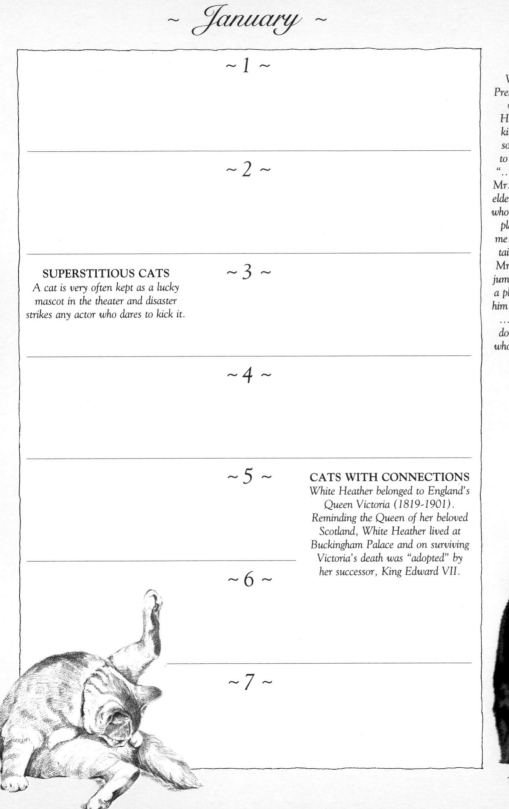

American Shorthairs are strong, muscular cats seen in many colors and coat patterns.

~ January ~

~ 8 ~

~ 9 ~

~ 10 ~

~ 11 ~

~ 12 ~

~ 14 ~

CARTOON CATS
George Herriman's Krazy Kat made his (or is it her?) debut in the New York Journal in 1910. Krazy became the star of the first cat comic strip, sharing stardom with the brickbat-throwing Ignatz Mouse.

RECORD-BREAKING CATS
Probably the oldest-known female cat was Ma, from Devon, England, who was 34 when she died in 1957.

CAT LEGENDS
There is a legend that many little kittens were thrown into a river to drown. The mother cat wept and was so distraught that the willows on the bank felt compassion and held out their branches to the struggling kittens who clung to them and were saved. Ever since that time, every spring, the willow wears gray buds that feel as soft and silky as the coats of little kittens. That is why they are called "pussy willows."

Ragdolls are an enchanting American breed.

Abyssinians produce on average 4 in a litter. Lively kittens grow into active, intelligent adults.

~ January ~

~ 15 ~

~ 16 ~

~ 17 ~

~ 18 ~

~ 19 ~

~ 20 ~

~ 21 ~

CAT SNIPS
When Calvin Coolidge was president in the 1920s, journalist Bascom Timmons insisted on taking his cat, Timmie, with him whenever he was summoned to the White House. The poor cat was hopelessly in love with Coolidge's canary, who, like the president on just about every issue, silently refused comment on the affair.

PERSONALITY CATS
Ernest Hemingway
Writer Ernest Hemingway had as many as 30 cats in his house and even allowed some of them to eat at the table with him. He may have been following the advice of his contemporary, the author Aldous Huxley, who once counseled a young man, "If you want to write, keep cats."

Stalking on the boardwalk.

CAT STARS
Orangey was a sensational motion picture and television personality. A veritable orange "tiger," Orangey made its cinematic debut in 1952 in the title role of "Rhubarb," and won the Patsy Award in 1952 and '62. Orangey also appeared in Gigot and Breakfast at Tiffany's, and the television series "Our Miss Brooks."

A cat with an agouti coat (when each hair is of two or three different colors) is well camouflaged in the undergrowth.

~ 22 ~

~ 23 ~

~ 24 ~

~ 25 ~

~ 26 ~

~ 27 ~

~ 28 ~

SUPERSTITIOUS CATS

Never kick a cat or you'll get rheumatism; never drown one or the devil will get you. Throughout the world it is considered bad luck to mistreat a cat. Such respect is probably rooted in those ancient religions in which the cat was a sacred animal and where retribution would befall anyone who harmed one.

PERSONALITY CATS

Desmond Morris
(b. January 24, 1928)
Zoologist, anthropologist, former Head of England's Granada TV and Film Unit at the Zoological Society of London, and Curator of Mammals at the London Zoo. Desmond Morris is now an author and host of TV programs specializing in cats, dogs, horses and other mammals. As a boy in the English countryside, he lived among many working cats, and they became an important part of his life.

Following the success of his book, The Naked Ape, the Morris family moved to the island of Malta where they were adopted by "a delightful cat" named Nimmo. They later returned to England and, following a trip to Africa to observe the "big cats," they found a little black cat at the top of an apple tree in their yard. They said hello in Swahili – which is "Jambo" – rescued the cat and adopted it. Jambo became its name and it stayed with the Morris family until its death 12 years later. Entirely black except for a tuft of white on its chest, Jambo was the source of Morris's more serious observations which led to his best-selling books, Catwatching *and* Catlore.

PERSONALITY CATS

Lewis Carroll
(b. January 27, 1832 –
d. January 14, 1898)
Born Charles Lutwidge Dodgson at Daresbury in the county of Cheshire, as Lewis Carroll he was the author of Alice In Wonderland *and* Alice Through the Looking Glass. *The former features the famous Cheshire Cat who had an uncomfortable habit of slowly disappearing – its smile being the last part to go!*

Cats are undeniably mysterious creatures.

The dense coat of the British Shorthair accentuates the handsome solidity for which it is known.

~ 29 ~

~ 30 ~

~ 31 ~

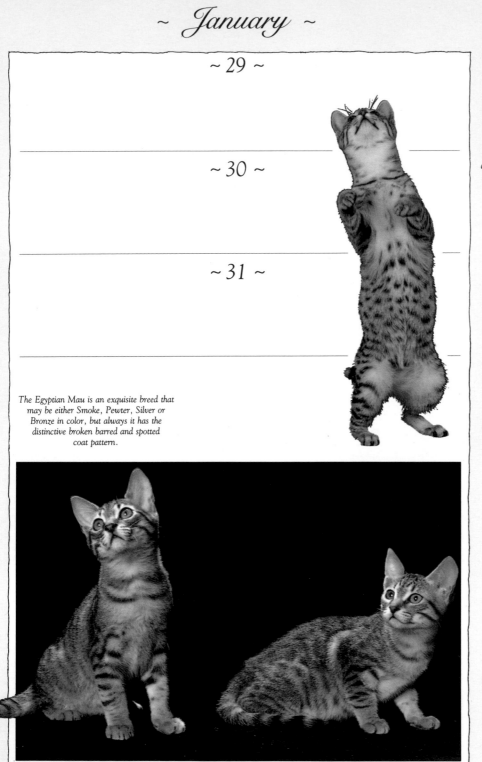

The Egyptian Mau is an exquisite breed that may be either Smoke, Pewter, Silver or Bronze in color, but always it has the distinctive broken barred and spotted coat pattern.

MYTHS & ORIGINS

The Egyptian Mau

In the beginning, the wild cat (felis vereata maniculata) was domesticated and the Egyptians called it Mau. The cat was greatly admired for its virility, ferocity and agility, and was sacred to the goddess Bast or Bastet – the center of whose cult was Bubastis on the Eastern Delta of the Nile. A fragment of papyrus from the XVIII Dynasty of ancient Egypt, dated around 1500 B.C., states that the male cat is Ra himself and that he was called Mau because of the speech of the god Sa who said: "He is like unto that which he hath made, therefore did the name of Ra become Mau." Accompanying the text is a painting of a cat holding a knife in one paw and the head of a slain serpent in another. Yet another myth tells of the "Great Cat of the Persea Tree" killing the serpent Apep.

Throughout the Bubastite Dynasty, the cat superseded all other animaux-derived religions and the cat goddess Bastet absorbed or smothered all rivals to and within the cult. In the domestic situation, the Mau was the subject of home worship while enjoying the role of adored pet, frequently adorned with jeweled necklaces and gold earrings. Favorite daughters in ancient Egypt were often given pet names which meant "little cat" of "kitten," or, more specifically "Mai-sheri," meaning Pussycat. In the 1950s, the only natural breed of the spotted domestic cat was seen at a cat show in Rome by the Princess Troubetsky. The Princess took one home with her to the U.S., and though immediate interest was shown, it was not until 1977 that the CFF (Cat Fanciers Federation) recognized the Egyptian Mau.

This Bronze Egyptian Mau possesses the breed's rounded wedge head, luminous green eyes and fine chin.

~ *February* ~

"*Seraphita remained for long hours immobile on a cushion, not sleeping,
following with her eyes with an extreme intensity of attention, scenes
invisible to simple mortals… Her elegance, her distinction, aroused the idea
of aristocracy; within her race, she was at least a duchess! She doted on
perfumes; with little spasms of pleasure she bit handkerchieves impregnated
with scent, she wandered among flasks on the dressing-table… and, if she
had been allowed to, would willingly have worn powder!*"

La Ménagerie Intime, Théophile Gautier, 1850

February cats are delightful, gentle creatures with an almost psychic intuitiveness and understanding.

~ February ~

~ 1 ~

~ 2 ~

~ 3 ~

~ 4 ~

~ 5 ~

~ 6 ~

~ 7 ~

SUPERSTITIOUS CATS

Matagots, or magician cats, are said to bring wealth to the home where they are well fed. According to French legend, a matagot must be lured by a plump chicken, then carried home without the prospective owner looking backward. Then, at each meal, the matagot must be given the first mouthful of food. In return, it will give its owner a gold coin each morning. In English legend, Dick Whittington, a poor boy who became Lord Mayor of London, owed his change of luck and his fortune to his cat, which was a matagot.

PERSONALITY CATS

Paul Gallico
(1897 – 1976)
The American novelist Paul Gallico celebrated his love for cats in his book, Honorable Cat, and confessed that he himself had an overabundance of them. But he pleaded guilty with an explanation: "Twenty-seven cats at one time hints at monomania, but in my case it was simpler. If you like cats and have some, you get kittens; and if you like kittens and enjoy having them about, they grow up and you get more cats."

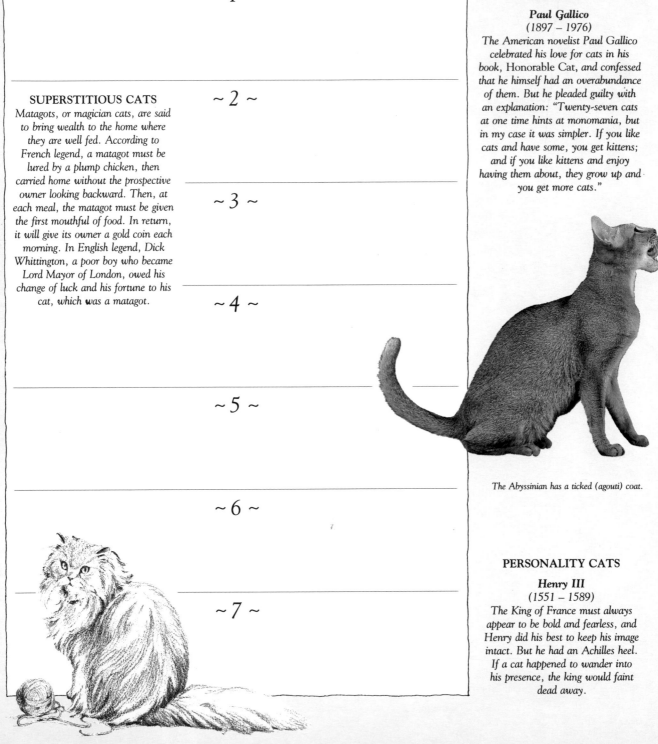

The Abyssinian has a ticked (agouti) coat.

PERSONALITY CATS

Henry III
(1551 – 1589)
The King of France must always appear to be bold and fearless, and Henry did his best to keep his image intact. But he had an Achilles heel. If a cat happened to wander into his presence, the king would faint dead away.

The Abyssinian, much admired for its slender grace, resembles the wild cat, felis lybica.

~ February ~

CAT SNIPS

The artist and author of nonsense verse, Edward Lear (1812-1888) was devoted to Foss, his tabby cat. His devotion was so great that when he decided to move to San Remo, Italy, he instructed his architect to design a replica of his old home in England so Foss would not be disturbed and suffer a minimum of distress after the move. Lear's drawings of his striped tabby cat are well-known, especially those which accompany his rhyme, "The Owl and the Pussycat."

~ 8 ~

~ 9 ~

~ 10 ~

~ 11 ~

~ 12 ~

~ 13 ~

~ 14 ~

Like an owl, the cat watches.

PRESIDENTIAL CATS

Born in 1809, Abraham Lincoln came to presidential office accompanied by Tabby, a cat belonging to his son, Tad Lincoln.

CAT SNIPS

"The cat is the animal to whom the Creator gave the biggest eye, the softest fur, the most supremely delicate nostrils, a mobile ear, an unrivaled paw and a curved claw borrowed from the rose tree…"

Colette

PERSONALITY CATS

Kim Novak
(b. February 13, 1933)
Born in Chicago, actress Kim Novak is famous for her starring role as a witch in the 1959 film, Bell, Book and Candle, in which her familiar was a seal point Siamese cat named Pyewacket.

Every big city has its population of stray and feral cats, adding to it their own particular feline charm.

~ February ~

~ 15 ~

~ 16 ~

CAT STARS
Pepper, a gray cat who lived in Hollywood, was a true motion picture "old timer" having worked with such classic silent movie greats as Charlie Chaplin, Fatty Arbuckle and the Keystone Kops.

~ 17 ~

CARTOON CATS
Garfield, the fat, lazy funny paper cat, was created by Jim Davis in 1978. Within four years, Garfield's comic strip was appearing in a thousand newspapers around the world.

~ 18 ~

~ 19 ~

~ 20 ~

~ 21 ~

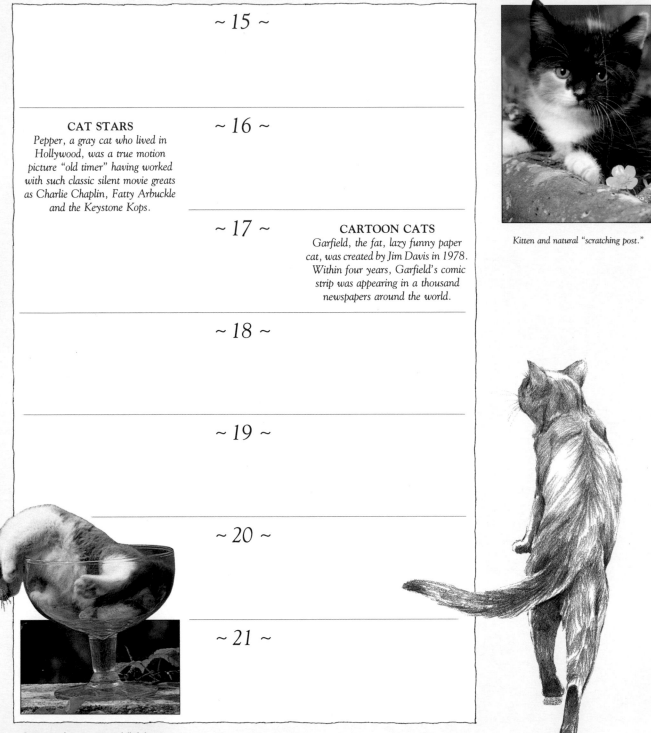

Kitten and natural "scratching post."

Just remember ... curiosity killed the cat.

Fastidious in their personal cleanliness, cats learn very young how to keep themselves in pristine condition.

~ 22 ~

~ 23 ~

SUPERSTITIOUS CATS

In Scotland in 1590, the warlock John Fian and members of his coven were charged with having raised, or attempting to raise, a storm to drown King James VI of Scotland (who survived to become James I of England), sailing home from Denmark. It was alleged that Fian and his accomplices attempted to create a storm by tossing cats into the sea.

~ 24 ~

~ 25 ~

The eyes reflect a cat's health.

CAT FACTS

The ancient Greeks don't seem to have shown much interest in cats. The Romans, on the other hand, were extremely fascinated by them and it was Caesar's legions that were largely responsible for introducing cats to the rest of Europe. In the fourth century A.D., *the domestic cat replaced the stone-marten as a rat killer in Rome. In France, the genet had been the animal used to control the rat population until the cat became the animal of choice in the 15th century.*

CAT SNIPS

Harry Cat, the hero of three books by George Seldon, lived in a drainpipe in New York's Times Square subway station with his pal, Tucker Mouse,

~ 26 ~

~ 27 ~

~ 28/29 ~

A cat on a healthy diet should never have any problems with its teeth or gums.

~ *March* ~

"*I conceived the idea that it would be well to hold Cat Shows, so that different breeds, colors, markings etc. might be more carefully attended to, and the domestic cat sitting in front of the fire would then possess a beauty and an attractiveness to its owner, unobserved and unknown because uncultivated before.*"

Our Cats, Harrison Weir, 1889

Harrison Weir organized the first cat show
in London at the Crystal Palace in 1871

The March cat is peace-loving and gentle and may seem to be in a world of his own for much of the time.

~ March ~

~ 1 ~

~ 2 ~

CARTOON CATS
"The Cat in The Hat," the creation of Theodor Seuss Geisel, who called himself "Dr. Seuss," first appeared in the children's book of the same name published in 1957.

~ 3 ~

~ 4 ~

SUPERSTITIOUS CATS
In what was known as Bohemia, now western Czechoslovakia, the cat was regarded as a symbol of fertility and it was believed that burying a cat in a field of grain guaranteed a good harvest.

~ 5 ~

~ 6 ~

~ 7 ~

PERSONALITY CATS

Charles Baudelaire
(b. 1821 – d. 1869)
The 19th-century French writer fully understood the mystique of the feline race when he said: " … chat mystérieux, chat séraphique, chat étrange."

Considered to be an eccentric in his complete empathy with every cat he met, Baudelaire devoted several poems to them in his Fleurs du Mal, and often felt that the cat was a spirit or a divinity which reigned over the household and asked: "Peut-être est-il fée, est-il dieu?" ("Is he perhaps a spirit, or god?")

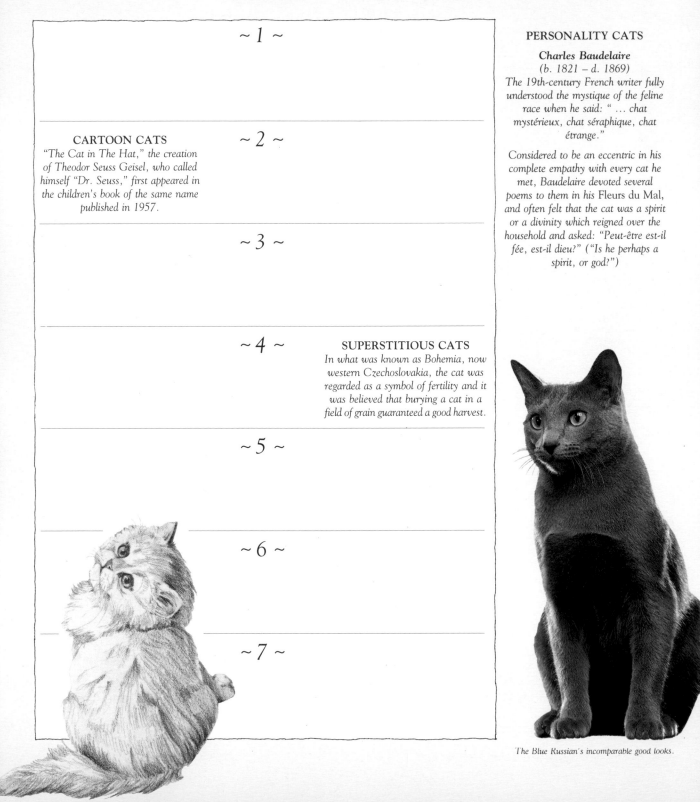

The Blue Russian's incomparable good looks.

Bright green, almond-shaped eyes, medium blue coats tipped with silver and small feet distinguish the Russian Blue.

~ March ~

~ 8 ~

CAT SNIPS

Chinese legend maintains that the cat is the product of a lioness and a monkey – the lioness endowing her offspring with dignity and the monkey with curiosity and playfulness.

~ 9 ~

SUPERSTITIOUS CATS

The Japanese prefer their own native short-tailed cat – the Japanese Bobtail – because it is less likely to "bewitch" humans. Japanese sailors have long taken tri-colored, or Mi-Ki, cats on their ships to bring them good luck. The figure of a cat with its left paw raised is commonly seen in gift shops in Japan where they are sold as souvenirs. It is believed that the beckoning cat brings good fortune to its owner.

~ 10 ~

~ 11 ~

~ 12 ~

~ 13 ~

~ 14 ~

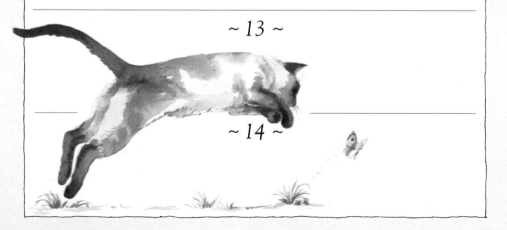

CAT SNIPS

A veterinarian who moved his practice from New York to California was forced to leave his cat behind, but five months later it appeared at the door of his new home, apparently none the worse for the wear of its nearly three-thousand-mile walk across the country. He knew it was the same cat because of an unmistakable scar from surgery he had performed himself several years earlier.

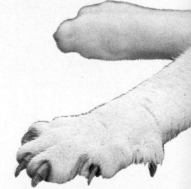

A delicate Japanese Bobtail. This coloring in the breed, known as Mi-Ki, is said to bring good fortune.

A unique and endearing characteristic of the cat is its purr, commonly thought to convey contentment, but unproven.

~ *March* ~

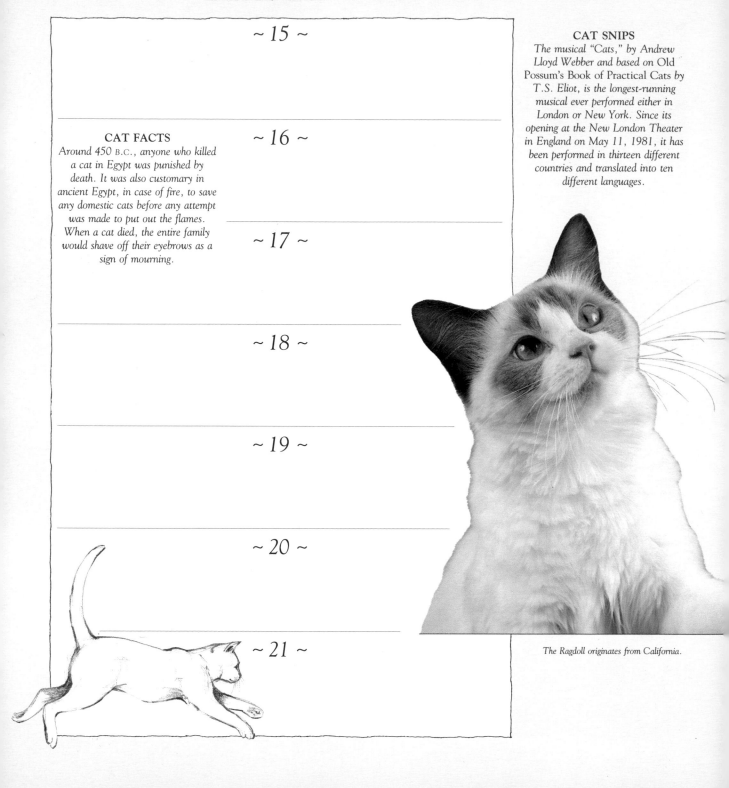

~ 15 ~

CAT FACTS
Around 450 B.C., anyone who killed a cat in Egypt was punished by death. It was also customary in ancient Egypt, in case of fire, to save any domestic cats before any attempt was made to put out the flames. When a cat died, the entire family would shave off their eyebrows as a sign of mourning.

~ 16 ~

~ 17 ~

~ 18 ~

~ 19 ~

~ 20 ~

~ 21 ~

CAT SNIPS
The musical "Cats," by Andrew Lloyd Webber and based on Old Possum's Book of Practical Cats by T.S. Eliot, is the longest-running musical ever performed either in London or New York. Since its opening at the New London Theater in England on May 11, 1981, it has been performed in thirteen different countries and translated into ten different languages.

The Ragdoll originates from California.

The Ragdoll, so named for its unique ability to relax completely when handled.

~ *March* ~

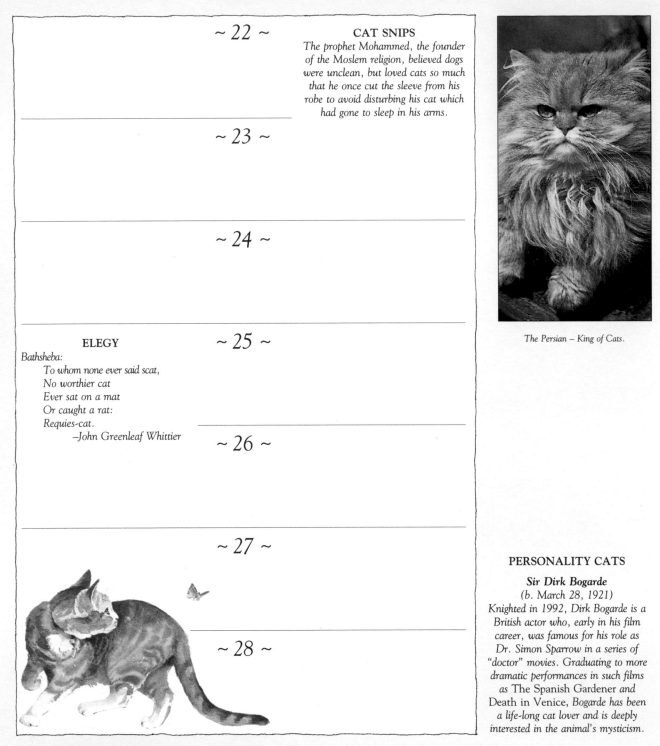

~ 22 ~

CAT SNIPS

The prophet Mohammed, the founder of the Moslem religion, believed dogs were unclean, but loved cats so much that he once cut the sleeve from his robe to avoid disturbing his cat which had gone to sleep in his arms.

~ 23 ~

~ 24 ~

The Persian – King of Cats.

ELEGY

Bathsheba:
To whom none ever said scat,
No worthier cat
Ever sat on a mat
Or caught a rat:
Requies-cat.
        —John Greenleaf Whittier

~ 25 ~

~ 26 ~

~ 27 ~

~ 28 ~

PERSONALITY CATS

Sir Dirk Bogarde
(b. March 28, 1921)
Knighted in 1992, Dirk Bogarde is a British actor who, early in his film career, was famous for his role as Dr. Simon Sparrow in a series of "doctor" movies. Graduating to more dramatic performances in such films as The Spanish Gardener *and* Death in Venice, *Bogarde has been a life-long cat lover and is deeply interested in the animal's mysticism.*

Occurring in Chinchilla Longhair litters for years, the Golden Persian gained formal recognition as a breed in 1983.

~ 29 ~

~ 30 ~

~ 31 ~

MYTHS & ORIGINS

Birman

Long before the teachings of Buddha enlightened the peoples of Asia, a temple was built high on the slopes of Mount Lugh by the Khmers of western Burma. The temple was called Lao Tsun, and it was there that the Kittah priests worshipped the golden, blue-eyed goddess Tsun-Kyan-Kse, to whose care the transmigration of souls was entrusted. The temple was guarded by many white long-haired cats with yellow eyes into whose bodies, according to Khmer belief, passed the souls of dead priests.

One such cat, whose name was Sinh, became the personal favorite of the High Priest Mun-Ha. One day, as Mun-Ha knelt to pray before the statue of the golden goddess, he was killed by invaders. Sinh leapt upon the body of its dead master and looked up into the sapphire eyes of the goddess. At that moment, the soul of the priest entered the body of the cat whose fur immediately took on the golden glow of the goddess and its eyes became a brilliant blue to match her own. Sinh's nose, ears, legs and tail darkened to take on the color of the earth but its paws, resting on the body of its dead master, remained white as a symbol of purity. Thus, the Birman, the sacred cat of Burma, came into being.

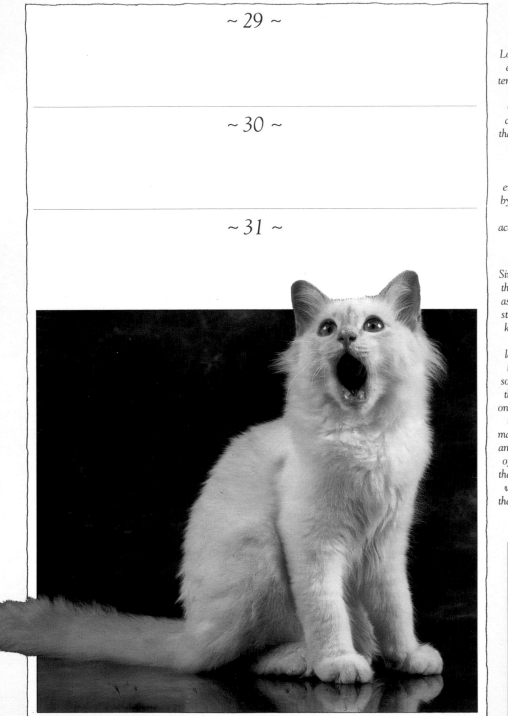

A Birman kitten's meow is music to any cat lover's ear.

Birmans have brilliant blue eyes.

Both good natured and beautiful, the Birman is an ideal house pet that gets along well with other animals.

~ *April* ~

"The male cat is Ra himself, and he was called Mau because of the speech
of the god Sa, who said concerning him: 'He is like unto that which he hath
made, therefore did the name of Ra become Mau.'"

Written on a fragment of papyrus from the XVIII Dynasty
of Ancient Egypt, c. 1500 B.C.

The April cat bursts with vitality and curiosity and therefore may be difficult to get in at night.

~ April ~

CAT FACTS

The Chinese knew the domestic cat before Europeans had ever heard of it, and the Japanese were not far behind them. In China and Japan the cat was used to protect silkworms from rodents, and Confucius himself was reported to have owned a cat, of whom he was very fond.

~ 1 ~

~ 2 ~

~ 3 ~

~ 4 ~

~ 5 ~

~ 6 ~

~ 7 ~

SUPERSTITIOUS CATS

Sailors believe that if a ship's cat mews and appears to be cross, they will face a hard voyage. But if the cat is bright and lively, they expect a brisk "following wind." It used to be said that a contrary wind at sea could be raised by shutting a cat in a canister, and that throwing a cat overboard resulted in an immediate storm. No sailor would ever dream of doing such a thing because it was considered bad luck to throw a cat overboard.

The Somali retains some wild characteristics

CAT SNIPS

Mr. Mephistopheles was the original conjuring cat from T. S. Eliot's Old Possum's Book of Practical Cats. A small, quiet black cat, it managed to produce seven kittens out of a hat.

The Somali is a long-haired Abyssinian sharing all its characteristics except in the voice, which is very quiet.

~ April ~

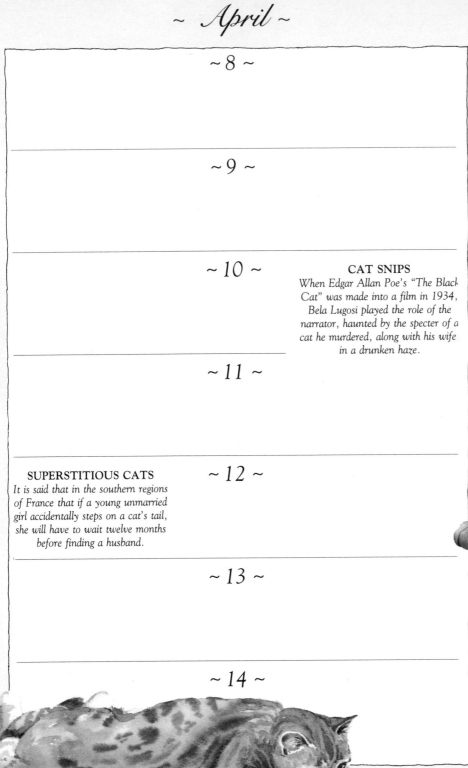

~ 8 ~

~ 9 ~

~ 10 ~

CAT SNIPS
When Edgar Allan Poe's "The Black Cat" was made into a film in 1934, Bela Lugosi played the role of the narrator, haunted by the specter of a cat he murdered, along with his wife, in a drunken haze.

~ 11 ~

SUPERSTITIOUS CATS
It is said that in the southern regions of France that if a young unmarried girl accidentally steps on a cat's tail, she will have to wait twelve months before finding a husband.

~ 12 ~

~ 13 ~

~ 14 ~

CAT SNIPS
Edgar Allan Poe (1809-1849), author of many macabre tales of mystery and imagination, was devoted to his tortoiseshell cat, Catarina. Poverty-stricken and unable to afford sufficient heat for his wife who lay dying of tuberculosis, Poe placed Catarina on the bed to keep his wife warm. The cat obligingly – or most probably mindful of its own comfort – stayed with the sick woman and, inspired by its loyalty, Poe was moved to write one of his best-known tales, "The Black Cat."

The Burmese, proud and full of grace.

These Abyssinian kittens display the breed's large tufted ears, rounded wedge-shaped heads and large, almond-shaped eyes.

~ 15 ~

~ 16 ~

CAT SNIPS

Non-pedigree cats generally live longer than pedigree cats. However, one pedigree cat reached its 31st birthday on April 17, 1989. It was Sukoo, a seal point Siamese who lived in the south of England, and was thought to be the oldest living pure-bred cat on record.

~ 17 ~

~ 18 ~

CAT HEROES

Naval hero cat Simon belonged to the captain of the British ship HMS Amethyst. When the vessel was bombarded by Chinese Communists on the Yangtse River on April 20, 1949, the captain and many of his crew were killed. Simon, suffering wounds and singed whiskers, kept at his post, killing off rats that had been frightened out of hiding by the shellfire. His prodigious catches were recorded by the awed crew, and on reaching Hong Kong, no one was surprised that Simon's fame had preceeded him and he was greeted with gifts, and letters and telegrams of congratulation. On returning to England, Simon pined away and was posthumously awarded the Dickin Medal, the animal equivalent of the Victoria Cross.

~ 19 ~

~ 20 ~

~ 21 ~

PERSONALITY CATS

Sir Kingsley Amis
(b. April 16, 1922)
Author, poet and intellectual, Kingsley Amis shares his London home with Sarah Snow, a graceful white cat with pale green eyes. With just slightly less than a semi-long coat and a hint of Angora in her ancestry, Sarah Snow is a gentle soul who likes to sit in the sun or doze by the radiator.

Author of such classics as Lucky Jim and The Old Devils, for which he was awarded the Booker Prize for Fiction in 1986, Kingsley Amis has lived surrounded by pets throughout his life – mainly both cats and dogs. Respecting a cat with intelligence, the author says "cats aren't as stupid as they often seem." Sarah Snow is obviously a cat in this category and Amis has written poems about their conversations. Despite venturing under floorboards with typical feline inquisitiveness and occasionally digging in her claws when sitting on her master's lap, Sarah Snow and Sir Kingsley Amis remain the very best of friends.

A threatening pose with bristling whiskers.

A cat will get lonely if left for any length of time, so a companion is often a good idea.

~ April ~

~ 22 ~

~ 23 ~

RECORD-BREAKING CATS
The largest recorded cat in Britain was a male named Poppa who died in 1985 weighing 44 pounds. Poppa lived in Gwent, Wales, and his average daily food intake consisted of one and a half cans of cat food, one can of evaporated milk and two handfuls of cat biscuits. Between meals, Poppa kept his strength up with leftover potatoes, cabbage, carrots and gravy and generous servings of home-made sponge cake.

~ 24 ~

~ 25 ~

CAT SNIPS
A black cat named Eponine was the pampered female companion of author Théophile Gautier. Pretty Eponine dined at the table with her master, partaking first of soup, then of fish, with all the delicacy of a well-mannered child.

~ 26 ~

~ 27 ~

~ 28 ~

SUPERSTITIOUS CATS
In the Middle Ages, cats were not very popular because of their association with witchcraft and black magic. Superstitions about cats, some of them current today, date back to this period. There are still people who believe that the cat is a reincarnation of the devil and regard it as bad luck if one crosses their path. In other places the reverse is held to be true, and that a black cat crossing one's path brings good luck.

The Bombay has a beautiful coat.

Perhaps this pussy is dreaming of going to sea with an owl in a beautiful pea-green boat.

~ *April* ~

~ 29 ~

~ 30 ~

Singapura
Possibly the smallest of the domestic cats, weighing about nine to fourteen pounds, the Singapura is a natural breed that originated on the island of Singapore. A free-ranging cat in its native land, the Singapura, with a smooth shorthaired agouti coat in its "natural" colors of ivory and brown became known as the "drain cat" because of its penchant for taking shelter in drain pipes. Following its registration with the Singapore Feline Society, the Singapura was exported to the United States in 1975 and shown a year later. Though still a rare breed, this quiet yet sociable little cat is found in various coat colors both in America and England.

Often a solitary creature, the cat is ingenious in his resourcefulness when making up games to play.

Known in its native country as the "Drain Cat," the elegant Singapur is a demure and affectionate cat.

~ *May* ~

"To gain the friendship of a cat is a difficult thing. The cat is a philosophical, methodical, quiet animal, tenacious of its own habits, fond of order and cleanliness, and it does not lightly confer its friendship. If you are worthy of its affection, a cat will be your friend, but never your slave. He keeps his free will, though he loves, and he will not do for you what he thinks unreasonable. But if he once gives himself to you it is with absolute confidence and affection!"

Théophile Gautier, 1850

May's cat loves his home and his food; the ideal pet for the loyal cat lover.

CAT STARS
In the 1979 movie Alien, *an orange-striped cat answering to the name "Jones" was one of only two survivors following the attack on the ship* Nostromo.

~ 1 ~

~ 2 ~

~ 3 ~

A playful rough and tumble.

CAT SNIPS
Philosopher Isaac Newton, famous for his laws of motion and gravity, was a confirmed cat lover who was deeply concerned about the welfare of his feline friends. Therefore, so that they should not feel restricted and be at liberty to wander freely in and out of the house when the doors were closed, he invented the cat-flap.

~ 4 ~

~ 5 ~

~ 6 ~

~ 7 ~

SUPERSTITIOUS CATS
A Celtic belief was that kittens born in May were badly behaved and troublesome. The Celts believed that the month of May was a time of ill-omen.

There is a certain sensuous delight in watching a cat at his langorous libations.

CAT SNIPS

In 1699, in a little town in Sweden, 300 children were accused of using demon cats to help them steal butter, bacon and cheese. Fifteen of the children were killed for the alleged crime and every Sunday during the following year thirty-six were whipped in front of the village church.

~ 8 ~

~ 9 ~

~ 10 ~

CAT SNIPS

King Charles I of England (1600-1649) owned a black cat that was his constant companion. He claimed that his pet brought him good luck and never went anywhere without it. When the cat finally died, the king was distraught and as he was mourning his lost luck, his enemies had him arrested and not long afterward, Charles I was beheaded.

~ 11 ~

~ 12 ~

~ 13 ~

~ 14 ~

Burmese & other Asians

The result of a "natural" mating, the brown shorthaired cat was, and is, known in Burma, now called Myanmar. The first of the "Burmese" cats were introduced to the Western world in 1930 when a female named Wong Mau arrived in New Orleans in the company of an American sailor. This "cobby" roundish type of cat was eventually given to Dr. Joseph C. Thompson of San Francisco, who decided to breed from the richly-hued brown feline. Illustrations of the Supalak or Thong Daeng – probable ancestors of the "foreigns," Burmese, Siamese and the Korat – can be seen in the Southeast Asian Cat Book Poems, produced between 1350 and 1750. This is possibly the oldest cat book in existence and reflects the high regard accorded to the cat in that place at that time.

Like all kittens, Burmese are irresistible

The Balinese is a long-haired mutation of the Siamese which first appeared in the 1950s.

~ *May* ~

~ 15 ~

~ 16 ~

~ 17 ~

~ 18 ~

~ 19 ~

~ 20 ~

~ 21 ~

SUPERSTITIOUS CATS

Occult powers are often attributed to cats. Some say they also have the power to hypnotize. According to one belief, a cat with three different colors in its coat protects humans from fire and fever.

CAT SNIPS

In 1785, the Swedish naturalist Carolus Linnaeus classified the domestic cat as felis catus. Since then, and understandably so, the animal has also been known as felis domesticus. The domestic cat flourished in ancient Egypt more than 2,500 years ago and, according to early Sanskrit writings, the cat was also domesticated in India at about the same time.

PERSONALITY CATS

James Mason
(b. May 15, 1909 – d. July 27, 1984)
James Mason was the darkly attractive British film star whose long Hollywood career made his voice and cultured accent an American standard. He was also well-known as an ailurophile, a cat lover, and along with his first wife, screenwriter Pamela Kellino, he owned several Siamese cats and provided a home for many strays. He and Ms. Kellino were the co-authors of The Cats in Our Lives, *published in 1949.*

Venice is home to many cats.

For animals known for their hatred of water, the cat has a peculiar affinity with Venice, city of canals.

CARTOON CATS

Felix the Cat, unlike other cartoon felines, began his career as a movie star rather than the subject of a newspaper cartoon. The creation of Australian-born Pat Sullivan, Felix was the star of the first "talkie" cartoon, a year before Mickey Mouse learned to talk. Felix was also the subject of one of the first experimental television broadcasts in 1928 and was NBC's official test pattern, helping engineers and viewers adjust the quality of their TV pictures until the late '30s.

PERSONALITY CATS

Sir Walter Scott
(1771 – 1832)

Scottish poet, novelist, editor and critic and deputy sheriff of Selkirk in 1799, just a few of Sir Walter Scott's better-known books are Rob Roy, The Talisman and Ivanhoe. Absorbed in folklore and the supernatural, Scott was devoted to cats, and a portrait of him by John Watson Gordon shows the author at work at his desk with his tabby, Hinx, lying close by. On the subject that fascinated him most, Scott wrote: "Cats are a mysterious kind of folk. There is more passing in their minds than we are aware of."

~ 22 ~

~ 23 ~

~ 24 ~

~ 25 ~

CAT QUOTES

"No matter how much cats fight, there always seems to be plenty of kittens."
– Abraham Lincoln

RECORD-BREAKING CATS

A Bonham, Texas, cat named Dusty gave birth to her 420th kitten in 1952. As though attempting to catch up, Bluebell of Wellington, South Africa, had a litter of fourteen kittens in 1974.

~ 26 ~

~ 27 ~

~ 28 ~

Cats can be very entertaining pets.

The Ocicat is well-muscled, graceful and lively, with tufted ears and large eyes set in a classic wedge-shaped head.

PRESIDENTIAL CATS

John F. Kennedy, born this day in 1917, was aided by a feline during his time in the White House. Tom Kitten, as it was called, actually belonged to Kennedy's daughter, Caroline, and was the first White House cat in more than fifty years, since the administration of Theodore Roosevelt. When Tom Kitten died, his newspaper obituary said: "Unlike many humans in the same position, he never wrote his memoirs of his days in the White House and never discussed them for quotation, though he was privy to many official secrets."

~ 29 ~

~ 30 ~

~ 31 ~

MYTHS & ORIGINS

Siamese

Legend has it that Siamese cats were kept to serve as repositories for the transmigrating souls of Siamese royalty. Residing only in the Royal Palace at Bangkok – hence their earlier name of Royal Palace Cat – it is said that they were the product of a union with an albino domestic cat and an Egyptian or, some say, a black Temple cat. The resulting "Siamese" were then appointed as guardians of the Temple and closely confined to keep the breed pure. Most early Siamese displayed one, two or three kinks in their tails. The myth of its origin is that a Siamese princess of long ago, while bathing, placed her rings on the tail of her favorite cat, which obligingly "kinked" it for that purpose. The squint, another inherent Siamese feature, is said to have originated when the priests of ancient Siam set the Palace cats to guarding a valuable vase. The cats carried out this duty for so long and with so much concentration that their eyes became permanently crossed.

In 1884, Owen Gould, the British Consul General in Bangkok was presented with a pair of Siamese cats by a member of the royal family. On his return to England, he gave the cats to his sister. A breeding pair, these strangely exciting animals were named Mia and Pho – Siamese for mother and father. More imports followed and in 1898, Wankee, a kitten stolen from the Royal Palace, became the first seal point Siamese to reach the status of Champion.

The Balinese cat's favorite food is fish, though this one seems to have a sweet tooth.

Cool and majestic, the Siamese is as distinctive as it is revered.

~ *June* ~

What does a kitten dream of ...?

Bright, nodding flowers;
Gay butterflies?
Sweet-scented grass;
Blue summer skies?

Cool woodland path
And dancing leaves?
Sunlight glinting
Through tall trees?

A puff of down
Gently touched by paw,
To float up and away
'Til seen no more?

The dreams of a kitten
Are gossamer things –
A slight hint of a breeze;
A faint rustle of wings ...

The dreams of a kitten
Are too precious to stay,
And as the fey mists of time,
They must melt away ...

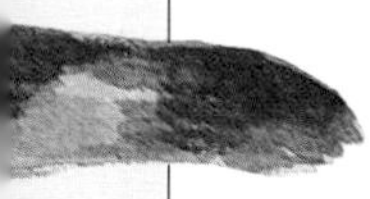

Anthology of Verse, Joan Moore, 1979

The June cat is energetic and intelligent, interested in everything and everyone, he hates being shut in.

~ June ~

A Persian chest as white as snow.

~ 1 ~

CAT SNIPS
The French astrologer, Nostradamus (1503-1566) posessed a cat named Grimalkin.

~ 2 ~

CAT NAPPING
After his election to the presidency, Bill Clinton's first negative encounter with the press came after photographers used catnip to lure his daughter Chelsea's cat, Socks, from their house for what is known as a photo opportunity. Clinton issued a stern warning, "Don't touch the cat again," and that, presumably, was that. But as The New York Times pointed out on its Editorial Page, Socks didn't need an executive order for protection. The Times said the cat "...did absolutely nothing to attract the world's attention. Further more, he will continue to do absolutely nothing. If guests at the White House hope to see him, he'll probably hide. Anyone who expects him to be cute on command has never met a cat. Despite his adoptive family's determined efforts to shield him from the press, Socks Clinton will stay famous all the time Chelsea Clinton's father is in office. Nonetheless, his will remain a cat's life: snoozing followed by eating followed by snoozing followed by pushing corks across the kitchen floor. At times he may be impelled to claw the leg of a chair. But he will never have to claw his way to the top."

~ 3 ~

~ 4 ~

CARTOON CATS
George Herriman, the creator of Krazy Kat, also provided the drawings for the three volumes of lower-case free verse composed by Don Marquis, but credited to Archy, a New York cockroach, in praise of Mehitabel, an alley cat with a human soul. Mehitabel claimed to have gone through a number of different incarnations before becoming a cat. It all began, she said, when she was Cleopatra.

~ 5 ~

~ 6 ~

~ 7 ~

The Blue Persian has a sumptuous coat of great length and density, dramatically offset by amber eyes.

CAT SNIPS

The cat is the only four-footed animal, with the exception of camels and giraffes, that walks by moving its front and hind legs first on one side and then on the other.

~ 8 ~

~ 9 ~

~ 10 ~

~ 11 ~

~ 12 ~

~ 13 ~

~ 14 ~

SUPERSTITIOUS CATS

An American hill-country superstition says that a cat can decide whether or not a girl should get married. The debating bride-to-be takes three hairs from a cat's tail and wraps them in a piece of paper, which she places under her door step. In the morning, if the cat hairs are aranged in a "Y" pattern, the answer is "Yes." But if the hairs form the letter "N," the answer is "No."

The Oriental has great sophistication.

CAT SNIPS

"Cats are distant, discreet, impeccably clean and able to stay silent. What more could be needed to be good company?"

Marie Leczinska (18th century)

It is as kittens at play that cats learn the skills of their species for hunting and survival.

~ June ~

CAT SNIPS

With powerful leg muscles, especially in its hind legs, the domestic cat has been known to reach running speeds of up to twenty-five miles an hour.

~ 15 ~

CAT SNIPS

When Adlai E. Stevenson, twice a presidential candidate, was Governor of Illinois in 1949, the State Legislature passed a law requiring cats to be kept on leashes. In his veto message, Governor Stevenson wrote: "I cannot agree that it should be the declared public policy of Illinois that a cat visiting a neighbor's yard or crossing the highway is a public nuisance. It is the nature of cats to do a certain amount of unescorted roaming. ... To escort a cat on a leash is against the nature of the cat. ... Moreover, cats perform useful service, particularly in rural areas. ... The problem of cat versus bird is as old as time. If we attempt to resolve it through legislation, who knows but what we may be called upon to take sides as well in the age-old problems of dog versus cat, bird versus bird or even bird versus worm. In my opinion, the State of Illinois and its local governing bodies have enough to do without trying to control feline delinquency."

~ 16 ~

SUPERSTITIOUS CATS

In an old Japanese folktale, a vampire transformed into a cat drained the blood of a beautiful maiden and was able to take on her form to bewitch the Royal Prince. The Prince was saved when the possessed woman was tracked down and ritually murdered.

~ 17 ~

~ 18 ~

CAT SNIPS

One of a cat's unwelcome habits is the clawing of furniture legs and upholstery. The animal is not sharpening its claws, but peeling away the covering (of the claws, not the furniture) to allow new growth to take place. Some cat owners "declaw" their pets, but usually only the front claws are removed, leaving the hind claws, the cat's real defensive weapon, intact.

~ 19 ~

~ 20 ~

~ 21 ~

Kittens get into lots of trouble.

A queen watches her kitten. By three or four weeks it will be on solids, by two months weaned.

~ June ~

~ 22 ~

~ 23 ~

~ 24 ~

~ 25 ~

~ 26 ~

~ 27 ~

~ 28 ~

SUPERSTITIOUS CATS

It is said that to dream of cats is unfavorable as this denotes treachery. In tasseography – fortune-telling by tea leaves – a cat signifies false friends and deceit; someone lies in treacherous ambush, probably a false friend.

CARTOON CATS

Sylvester, the animated cartoon character, first appeared in the "Life With Feathers" television cartoon in 1945.

CAT SNIPS

Written by an Irish monk in the margin of an illuminated manuscript at the Abbey of St. Paul at Reichenau, Carinthia, around the eighth century is a short poem that begins: "I and Pangur Ban, my cat. Hunting mice is his delight …" It later inspired a book telling of the adventures of Pangur Ban who finally ended his travels at Cashel Castle in Ireland, where he was greatly loved for keeping it rodent-free. Pangur Ban is Gaelic for "little white cat."

A white Persian is a precious creature.

The sleep of a cat is much coveted for its blameless ease and disconcern.

~ 29 ~

~ 30 ~

CAT QUOTES
"When I play with my cat, who
knows whether she is not amusing
herself with me more than I with her?"

Michel de Montaigne (1533-1592)

CAT QUOTES
"No man has ever dared manifest his
boredom so insolently as does the
Siamese tomcat when he yawns in
the face of his amorously importunate
wife. No man has ever dared to
proclaim his illicit amours so frankly
as this same tom caterwauling on
the tiles."

Aldous Huxley (1894-1963)

What dreams of mice and fish stir in the slumbers of these napping cats?

When not sleeping, a cat is often grooming, a lengthy process of meticulous care and seriousness.

~ *July* ~

"The Egyptians have observed in the eyes of a Cat, the encrease of the Moonlight for with the Moone, they shine more fully at the full, and more dimly in the change and wain, and the male Cat doth also vary his eyes with the Sunne; for when the Sunne ariseth, the apple of his eye is long; towards noone it is round, and at the evening it cannot be seene at all, but the whole eye sheweth alike."

Historie of Foure-footed Beasts, Edward Topsel, 1607

The July cat thrives on affection and repays it generously. It makes an excellent parent and devoted pet.

~ *July* ~

~ 1 ~

~ 2 ~

The stalking Bombay is formidable.

SUPERSTITIOUS CATS
Many people believe that a black cat brings good fortune and also that anyone who finds the one perfect white hair on an all-black cat and plucks it out without being scratched will find great wealth and good luck in love.

~ 3 ~

~ 4 ~

IDEA
Isn't it about time we set aside a national holiday to celebrate cats? And can you think of a better day than this? It's Independence Day! Write your Congressman!

CAT LEGENDS
Typhon, from whom our word "typhoon" originates, was a fearsome creature whose fiery breath caused great destruction in the world. It was its custom to roar over land and sea, raising fierce storms and destroying everything in its path. Its ambition was to gain sovereignty, not only over mankind, but over the gods also. So nearly did Typhon succeed in attaining its ambition that gods and goddesses hid from it by taking the form of animals. Hecate, a mysterious divinity whom the ancients identified with the night and who associated with ghosts and demons, was said to be an expert at magic, adopted the shape of a cat until Zeus destroyed the giant Typhon with a thunderbolt. Thereafter, although she resumed her proper form, Hecate had a special affection for cats. She became the patron saint of witches – as Shakespeare noted when he made his "dark and midnight hags" appeal to her for help in ruining Macbeth. It followed naturally for those who practiced witchcraft to cultivate an affection for cats.

~ 5 ~

~ 6 ~

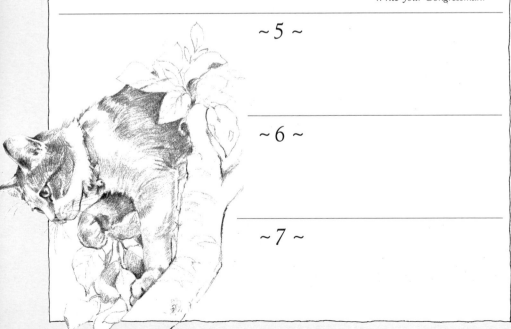

~ 7 ~

A "comfort" of cats. Two of a kind curl up together.

~ 8 ~

~ 9 ~

~ 10 ~

~ 11 ~

~ 12 ~

~ 13 ~

~ 14 ~

CAT SNIPS

Williamina, a white cat belonging to the 19th-century English author, Charles Dickens, was originally named William, but was renamed when he revealed himself to be a she by producing a litter of kittens. Because of its devotion to the author, one kitten was not offered for adoption but became a member of the Dickens household where it regularly signaled the end of the workday by snuffing out on the candle on the writing table with its paw. Dickens usually took the hint and complied with a cuddle for his favorite cat.

Pretty maids all in a row.

CAT SNIPS

Difficult as it is to believe, not everyone loves cats. Genghis Kahn was a famous cat-hater and so were Alexander the Great and Julius Caesar. It may be that men with dreams to dominate the world can't get used to the idea that cats won't submit to them. The same streak of ailurophobia affected the personalities of Napoleon Bonaparte, Adolf Hitler and Benito Mussolini.

PRESIDENTIAL CATS

Gerald Ford, born on this day, was privileged to have Shan as the First Cat of his administration. The Siamese belonged to President Ford's daughter, Susan.

The white Shorthair is a most delightful cat, particularly when odd-eyed. The blue-eyed variety can suffer from deafness.

CAT LEGENDS

The ancient Romans believed that the cat was created by the goddess Diana, and that it was really just a joke. According to the story, Apollo, in a mood for showing off, created the lion and to mock him, Diana created a miniature of his creation: a pussycat.

~ 15 ~

~ 16 ~

~ 17 ~

~ 18 ~

~ 19 ~

~ 20 ~

~ 21 ~

CAT SNIPS

The average life span of a cat is twelve years and it is said that to compare the age of a cat to that of a human, simply multiply the cat's age by seven. On the other hand, puberty in females can occur at six months, so be careful not to assume that the formula means you won't have kittens until your cat approaches the age of two.

The Chartreux has orange or copper eyes.

PERSONALITY CATS

Ernest Hemingway
(b. July 21, 1898 – d. July 2, 1961)
A former war correspondent who covered the Spanish Civil War and later a successful novelist who won the Nobel Prize for Literature in 1954 and the Pulitzer Prize for his Old Man and The Sea in 1953. When he lived in Paris with his wife and young son, he would leave F. Puss, his yellow-eyed cat, to baby-sit for them. Consternation was rife among their friends and neighbors, who feared that the cat would lie on the baby and suffocate him. But not F. Puss; the careful cat sat upright and on guard until the parents returned.

With novels such as To Have and Have Not, The Snows of Kilimanjaro and For Whom the Bell Tolls, to his credit, Hemingway discussing his favorite subject said: "The cat has complete emotional honesty, an attribute not often found in humans."

Keeping a long-haired cat in perfect condition requires daily grooming and the occasional bath.

CAT SNIPS

In New York in 1963, a Chinchilla Persian Longhair called Babyface and a Silver Persian Longhair named Nicodemus were married. The ceremony was conducted by a beagle and the Matron-of-Honor was another Persian cat.

~ 22 ~

~ 23 ~

CAT STARS

"That Darn Cat," was a fictional feline portrayed by Syn Cat, the star of the 1964 Walt Disney film that also featured Dean Jones, Hayley Mills, Roddy McDowell, Frank Gorshin and William Demarest.

~ 24 ~

~ 25 ~

~ 26 ~

~ 27 ~

~ 28 ~

PERSONALITY CATS

Raymond Chandler
*(b. July 23, 1888 –
d. March 26, 1959)*
Born in Chicago, Raymond Chandler was famous for his series of detective stories featuring private eye, Philip Marlowe. Chandler created the classic detective novel form popular in the 1930s and '40s and many of his books became successful movies, notably The Big Sleep, starring Humphrey Bogart and Lauren Bacall. A lifelong cat devotee, Chandler owned a black Persian named Taki, whom he called his "feline secretary," because she would sit on his manuscripts while he worked and then move the pages out of his reach.

The Smoky Persian is very luxuriant.

The Chinchilla Longhair has large, expressive emerald-green eyes outlined in black or brown.

~ 29 ~

~ 30 ~

~ 31 ~

MYTHS & LEGENDS

Korat

Si-Sawat – meaning good fortune – is the name given to the Korat in its native Thailand. Much prized for their beauty, these sweet-tempered cats were described in ancient Thai manuscripts. Created by artists and writers of the Ayudha period (A.D.1350-1767) they tell of a blue cat having "hairs so smooth with roots like clouds and tips like silver," and "eyes that shine like dewdrops on a lotus leaf." The clear, luminous eyes of the Korat are part of its mystique: "These cloud-colored cats with eyes the color of young rice…"

Symbols of good luck, Korats were often given to brides to insure a happy and prosperous future. Originating hundreds of years ago in the Korat Province of Siam, now known as Thailand, the Korat today still possesses the same compact, muscular body, blue silver-tipped coat and sparkling green eyes that intrigued and enchanted its countrymen all those years ago… The coat of some Korats, however, is of a deeper hue that is almost indigo. These rare and very special cats are known as "black pearls."

Then as now, the Korat had a gentle nature with a marked dislike of noise. Their very sensitive hearing prompted the Siamese to place them as "watch cats" in their temples to guard the valuable treasures there.

After the Korat was introduced into the West, judges in the 1896 National Cat Club Show in London disqualified the cat from the Siamese division because it was "blue instead of biscuit colored." The owner protested that not only had the cat come from Siam, but that there were many others like it. There was some confusion surrounding the "blue Siamese" for several years after that, and it wasn't until 1959 that the Korat received international recognition when a pair named Nara and Dara were taken to the United States from Bangkok and officially registered.

A rare and exotic breed, the Korat is silver-blue in color and has large, luminous green eyes.

~ *August* ~

"The cat makes himself the companion of your hours of solitude,
melancholy and toil. He remains for whole evenings on your knee, uttering
his contented purr, happy to be with you and forsaking the company of animals o
his own species. In vain do melodious mewings on the roof invite him to one of
those cat parties in which fish bones play the part of tea and cakes; he is not to
be tempted away from you. Put him down and he will jump up again, with a
sort of cooing sound that is like a gentle reproach; and sometimes he will sit upon
the carpet in front of you, looking at you with eyes so melting, so caressing, so
human, that they almost frighten you; for it is impossible to believe
that a soul is not there."

Théophile Gautier, 1850

August's cat is bold and proud with a big heart, and makes a loyal and generous companion.

~ August ~

~ 1 ~

~ 2 ~

~ 3 ~

~ 4 ~

~ 5 ~

~ 6 ~

~ 7 ~

CAT STARS
One of the most famous cats in America is Morris, a fourteen-pound orange charmer who was rescued from a Chicago animal shelter, just as he was about to be destroyed, by trainer Bob Martwick. Morris became the spokes-cat for 9-Lives cat food in 1969, and eventually became an honorary director of Star-Kist Foods, with veto power over any cat food flavor he didn't like. When President Richard Nixon signed an animal-protection bill into law, Morris was invited to co-sign it with his paw-print. Up until the time he died in 1978, the cat lived in a Chicago dog kennel where there was never, ever, any question about who was boss.

CAT SNIPS
*Cruel, but composed and bland,
Dumb, inscrutable and grand,
So Tiberius might have sat
Had Tiberius been a cat.*

Matthew Arnold (1822-1888)

CAT SHOWS
The first organized cat show in the United States was held in New York in 1895, but the first one considered important took place in Chicago four years later. It has become traditional to hold such affairs between September and February, a time when a cat's coat seems to reach a kind of peak. It is also a lull in the breeding season for females and cooler temperatures make the males a good deal less fiesty. Unaltered kittens less than eight months old frequently compete in cat shows, and the usual categories of competition for older cats are Non-Championship, which includes a subdivision known as AOV (Any Other Variety) that covers cats either difficult to classify or not quite purebred; Premiereship, reserved for neutered cats; and Championship.

The most special prizes of all are reserved for the Champions, and that category is usually broken down into competitions among "Novices" who have never won a ribbon; the so-called "Open" for cats on the verge of championship; the Champion class for those a little further up the line; and, finally, Grand Champion, the contest to find the true king (or queen) of the beasts.

Kittens at play are very amusing.

For show purposes, the Bicolor Persian should have evenly-distributed colored patches with clear white patches to include the underside.

CAT SNIPS

The trouble with a kitten is
THAT
Eventually it becomes a
CAT

Ogden Nash (1902-1971)

~ 8 ~

~ 9 ~

~ 10 ~

CAT LEGENDS

A legend relates that when Noah built his Ark, he had two of every animal except the domestic cat, which was unknown in his time. The rain began to fall and the rats began to multiply and raid the Ark's store of provisions. In despair, Noah asked the lion for advice. The lion thought, scratched its head and sneezed, whereupon two small lions jumped out of its nostrils. These were the very first cats and they immediately began hunting, quickly diminishing the number of rats and mice.

~ 11 ~

~ 12 ~

CARTOON CATS

Figaro, a kitten fascinated by puppet-maker Gepetto's goldfish, Cleo, was created for Walt Disney's full-length animated film Pinocchio in 1940.

~ 13 ~

~ 14 ~

The ever-appealing Abyssinian.

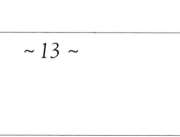

Most cats keep their claws in good condition by "stropping" them on trees or scratching posts. Others may need to have their claws clipped.

~ 15 ~

~ 16 ~

CAT STARS
Solomon was a Chinchilla longhair who became a movie star in such films as Diamond are Forever *and* A Clockwork Orange.

~ 17 ~

~ 18 ~

CAT FACTS
In ancient Egypt, the male cat represented the Sun and the female cat the Moon.

~ 19 ~

~ 20 ~

~ 21 ~

A Persian in deserved prime position.

CAT SNIPS
The origin of the Cheshire Cat in Lewis Carroll's Alice in Wonderland *is somewhat ambiguous, but there are two sources on which the author, born in Cheshire, England, may have based the character of his famous disappearing cat. One concerns the Cheshire town of Congleton, where a ghostly cat unpredictably appeared and disappeared, a phenonomenon witness by many townsfolk in the last century. The second possibility is a medieval tale from the City of Chester, wherein lived one John Catterall, a landowner who was also a forester. His skill with an axe made him ideal for the post of Public Executioner and Caterall gained fame for the manner in which he dispatched the condemned – with a wide grin on his face. Appropriately, his coat of arms included a grinning cat.*

In Britain, the Chinchilla differs from other Persians in that it is slightly more fine-boned, though it is no less hardy.

~ August ~

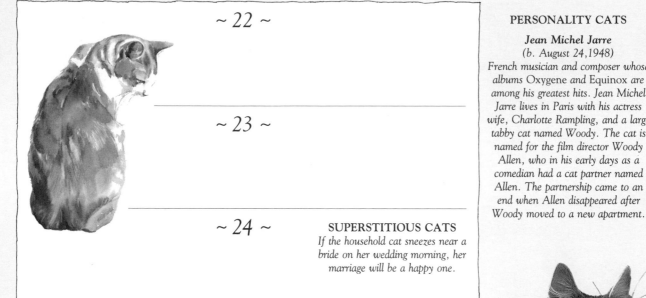

~ 22 ~

~ 23 ~

~ 24 ~

SUPERSTITIOUS CATS
If the household cat sneezes near a bride on her wedding morning, her marriage will be a happy one.

~ 25 ~

CAT SNIPS
"In the event of an air raid, don't worry about your cats. Cats can take care of themselves far better than you can. Your cat will probably meet you as you enter the air raid shelter."

Advice supplied by the British Broadcasting Corporation to Londoners in 1939.

~ 26 ~

~ 27 ~

~ 28 ~

PERSONALITY CATS

Jean Michel Jarre
(b. August 24, 1948)
French musician and composer whose albums Oxygene and Equinox are among his greatest hits. Jean Michel Jarre lives in Paris with his actress wife, Charlotte Rampling, and a large tabby cat named Woody. The cat is named for the film director Woody Allen, who in his early days as a comedian had a cat partner named Allen. The partnership came to an end when Allen disappeared after Woody moved to a new apartment.

A fine example of the tabby.

"Paws for thought," and a little nap on a cool flagstone.

~ 29 ~

~ 30 ~

~ 31 ~

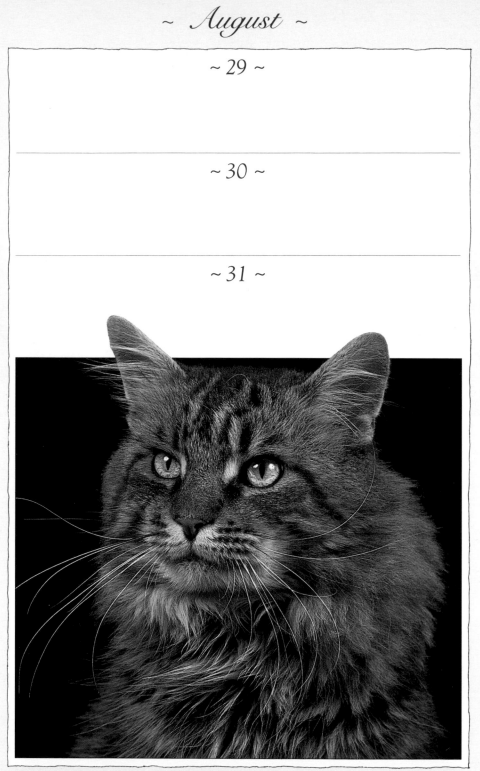

CAT BREEDS

Maine Coon
One of the oldest breeds in America, the Main Coon originated in the State of Maine and was first recorded in 1861 with the mention of one called "Captain Jinks." Thought to be the result of matings between the Angora and Maine working cats, local folklore has it that, because of its dark tabby coat and bushy tail, that semi-wild cats mated with raccoons – hence the name, Maine Coon. Not unlike the Norwegian forest cat, the Maine Coon is a hardy cat with a shaggy longhaired coat. It is also one of the largest of all cat breeds, weighing between eleven and fifteen pounds. One example was said to have weighed forty pounds! First exhibited in America in 1895, the Maine Coon is now a popular breed in both the United States and Britain.

According to American folklore, the impressive Main Coon is the result of a semi-wild cat and a raccoon mating.

A beautiful Maine Coon with the breed's distinctively high cheek bones and pointed, tufted ears.

~ September ~

"Those fortunate enough to have been touched by its mystique will agree that once the strange Oriental magic of the Siamese cat has been revealed to them, they will forever remain in its enchanted spell..."

The Fabulous Siamese, Joan Moore, 1986

September's cat is fastidiously clean and hygienic and is not averse to its own company – the classic cat.

~ September ~

Strong and massive, the handsome Chartreux.

~ 1 ~

~ 2 ~

~ 3 ~

~ 4 ~

~ 5 ~

~ 6 ~

~ 7 ~

CAT FACTS
Russian history tells us that long ago in a magnificent palace at St. Petersburg, three hundred cats were kept to hunt and kill the mice that might otherwise destroy the many priceless leather-bound books that were stored in its library.

CAT SNIPS
Valued highly for the services to man, cats in fifth-century China were often given the name Tama, meaning "jewel."

PERSONALITY CATS

Colette
(b. 1873 – d. 1954)
A French authoress who adored cats, Colette wrote Claudine, *a semi-autobiographical series of novels, and also* Cheri *in 1920. In* La Chatte *(1933) she describes the tortures of jealousy when a young husband has eyes, and arms, only for Saha, his beloved cat. Camilla, the wife, seeks to destroy the object of her husband's passion, and fails, only to lose her husband forever. Saha, the story's feline heroine, is based on La Chatte, the cat which Colette shared with her husband, Maurice Goudeket. The cat, a Chartreux, was a delightful creature with a plushy blue coat and yellow eyes who adopted the writer at a cat show.*

The many cats in Colette's works include the pampered La Belle Franchette, Babou, a black cat with a penchant for fruit and vegetables from the kitchen garden; her own Angora, Kiki-la-Doucette and the French bulldog Toby-Chien. "Dialogue des Betes" was a collection of conversations between these two pets. Colette, the flamboyant cat lover who posed as the Sphinx in a photograph considered daring and controversial, said, "There are no ordinary cats."

Virtually the same as the British Blue Shorthair, the Chartreux has a slightly more grayish blue coat.

~ September ~

LITERARY CATS
In Mark Twain's novel, Tom Sawyer, Tom meets his friend Huckleberry Finn carrying a dead cat. "What dead cats good for?" asks Tom. "Cure warts with," says Huck, who continues: "Why, you take your cat to a graveyard 'long about midnight when somebody that was wicked has been buried; and when it's midnight a devil will come, or maybe two or three, but you can't see 'em, you can only hear something like the wind, or maybe hear 'em talk; and when they're taking that feller away, you heave your cat after 'em and say, 'Devil follow corpse, cat follow devil, warts follow cat, I'm done with ye!' That'll fetch any wart."

~ 8 ~

~ 9 ~

~ 10 ~

~ 11 ~

~ 12 ~

~ 13 ~

~ 14 ~

Kittens are irrepressibly curious.

Contact is very important for kittens.

CAT SNIPS
French missionaries first introduced domestic cats into North America as gifts of friendship to the Huron Indians, who were unimpressed. English colonists were also apparently unimpressed by cats and it wasn't until 1749 when the Pennsylvania Colony was overrun by rats that cats were imported from Europe. Today there are nearly forty million cats in the United States, about double the number of dogs.

CAT QUOTES
"Nothing is more playful than a young cat, nor more grave than an old one."

Thomas Fuller (1608-1661)

At about a month of age a kitten, like a toddling child, will be in and out of everything.

~ 15 ~

~ 16 ~

~ 17 ~

~ 18 ~

~ 19 ~

~ 20 ~

~ 21 ~

CAT SNIPS

Cardinal Richelieu (1586-1642) was so fond of cats that he shared his home with fourteen of them. Their names included Pyramé, Thisbe, Lucifer and Perruque. Specially appointed attendants cared for the cats and on his death, the cardinal left all his worldly wealth to his feline friends.

CAT SNIPS

French researchers claim that the average cat has a vocal range of as many as sixty notes, from a gentle purr to growls of varying intensity to the howls that sometimes annoys the neighbors. On the island of Java, people imitate some of those notes with a musical instrument called the saron, a percussion instrument shaped like a cat whose sound is made by stroking slats on its back.

SUPERSTITIOUS CATS

In Britain, along the Yorkshire coast, wives of fishermen believe that their menfolk will return safely if a black cat is kept in the house.

The Tonkinese is a cross between a Siamese and a Burmese, developed in America in the 1970s.

~ September ~

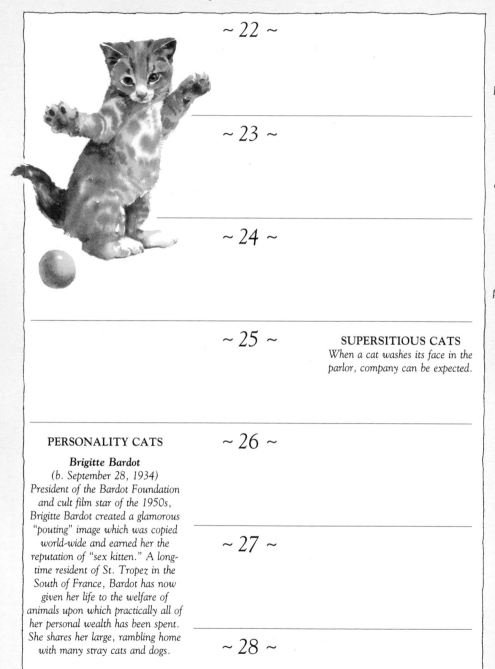

~ 22 ~

~ 23 ~

~ 24 ~

~ 25 ~

SUPERSITIOUS CATS

When a cat washes its face in the parlor, company can be expected.

~ 26 ~

PERSONALITY CATS

Brigitte Bardot
(b. September 28, 1934)
President of the Bardot Foundation and cult film star of the 1950s, Brigitte Bardot created a glamorous "pouting" image which was copied world-wide and earned her the reputation of "sex kitten." A long-time resident of St. Tropez in the South of France, Bardot has now given her life to the welfare of animals upon which practically all of her personal wealth has been spent. She shares her large, rambling home with many stray cats and dogs.

~ 27 ~

~ 28 ~

PERSONALITY CATS

T. S. Eliot
(b. September 26, 1888 –
d. January 4, 1965)
Born in St. Louis, Missouri, Thomas Stearns Eliot was the youngest of seven children in a family that had emigrated from England in the 17th century. Educated at Harvard University, the Sorbonne in Paris and Oxford in England, T.S. Eliot eventually settled in Britain where he met his countryman, the poet Ezra Pound who encouraged him to write plays. Eliot's best-known play was Murder in the Cathedral, commissioned for the 1935 Canterbury Festival. Equally well-known was the reflection of his passion for cats, Old Possum's Book of Practical Cats, which eventually became the inspiration for the musical, Cats.

Eliot's wife, Valerie, recalls that he especially enjoyed inventing suitable cat names for the book, including Noilly Prat, an elegant cat, and Tantomile, a witch's cat. The book, first published in 1939, included Eliot's own drawings on the front cover. It became a world-wide best-seller, translated into many different languages. T.S. Eliot was awarded the Nobel Prize for literature in 1948.

A proud Persian of great charisma.

The Red and White Bicolor Longhair's disarmingly open gaze makes it quite irresistible.

~ 29 ~

~ 30 ~

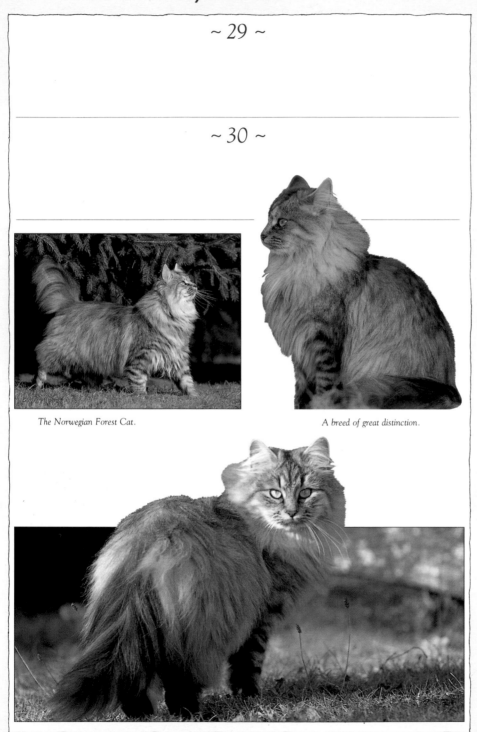

The Norwegian Forest Cat.

A breed of great distinction.

Used to harsh Scandinavian winters, this cat has a thick double coat.

MYTHS & ORIGINS

Norwegian Forest Cat

An active, athletic cat giving the impression of great power and strength, the Norwegian forest cat is a natural breed which figures prominently in Scandinavian folklore. It is said that long, long ago this large and fearsome cat of the northern forests was taken by the Vikings to guard their homes and to live with families as vermin hunter and household pet. It is also said that these longhaired cats were carried on the shoulders of Viking warriors to attack and claw the faces of their enemies. Many old Scandinavian folk tales, though often confused and compounded, featured these felines who were greatly respected by the Norsemen for their strength and agility. That the marauding Vikings took these cats on their voyages to the known world and beyond is also held to be true. As the Norwegian forest cat bears a strong resemblance to the American Maine Coon, this could indicate the extent of the sea-going forays of the Norsemen.

In Norse mythology, the chariot of Freya, goddess of beauty, love and fertility, is drawn by two large longhaired cats; these creatures are often connected with the powers of creativity, the Earth Mother and fertility gods. Also connected with Freya is Utgard-Loki, King of the Giants, who also had a giant cat. The Norwegian forest cat, or Norsk Skaukatt, is probably the main character of the Scandinavian version of "Puss in Boots," in which the ogre is a troll, which dies in sunlight. To help its master, this resourceful puss kept the troll chatting throughout the night until the early morning sun destroyed him.

Similar in appearance to the Maine Coon, the Norwegian Forest Cat may be of various colors.

~ *October* ~

"When we go into the likeness of a cat, we say thrice over:

'I shall go into a cat,
With sorrow and a sigh and a black shot.
I shall go in the Devil's name
Ay, while I come home again.'"

Magick Spell used for Metamorphosis as described by the witch
Isabel Gowdie at her trial in Scotland in 1662

October's cat loves the finer things in life, like soft cushions, gentle music and constant shows of affection.

PRESIDENTIAL CATS

Born on October 1, 1924, when Jimmy Carter became president, his life was enhanced by the presence of Misty Malarky Ying Yang, a male Siamese belonging to his daughter, Amy.

CAT SNIPS

A sensible quote from 19th-century British cat expert Frances Simpson discussing the newly imported Siamese breed: "Siamese are a special breed and should be kept as such. The same may be said of the Manx and the Blues. All attempts to cross these cats with other breeds should be discouraged."

~ 1 ~

~ 2 ~

CAT FACTS

The cat's skeleton is quite close to that of humans, but its lack of a shoulder blade allows freedom of movement of the foreleg, which can be turned in almost any direction.

~ 3 ~

~ 4 ~

A fine litter of Birman kittens.

~ 5 ~

SUPERSTITIOUS CATS

It is said that a cat looking out of the window is looking for rain.

~ 6 ~

~ 7 ~

The appealing face of the Siamese.

The quintessential Siamese – the seal point. The pale fawn to cream body is marked at the tail, feet, legs, mask and ears.

~ October ~

A cat makes a home.

~ 8 ~

~ 9 ~

~ 10 ~

~ 11 ~

SUPERSTITIOUS CATS
In some parts of the United States, black and white and also gray cats are considered to be lucky.

CAT FACTS
The name "tabby," used to describe the markings of a striped or brindled cat, comes from the name of the Attibiah district of Baghdad. Jews living there once made a high-quality silk with black and white watery pattern. Exported to Britain, the fabric became known as "tabbi" silk.

~ 12 ~

~ 13 ~

~ 14 ~

CAT SNIPS
Kasper is a wooden black cat designed by Basil Ionides in 1916. It stands on a shelf in the Pinafore Room of London's prestigious Savoy Hotel. When guests at a luncheon or dinner party number thirteen, Kasper is seated in a fourteenth chair to confound the superstition that thirteen is an unlucky number. Sir Winston Churchill, who frequently entertained in the room, dined with Kasper many times.

Shampooed, groomed and back-lit, this Persian has been bred for stardom.

CAT STARS

MTM Kitten is the corporate symbol of the television production company, Mary Tyler Moore Enterprises. The little tabby, which doesn't have a name, has been the signature of the company's programs since 1970. It is a parody of Leo the Lion, which has been adding its roar of approval to movies made by Metro-Goldwyn-Mayer since the 1930s.

The very elegant Cat of Bengal.

~ 15 ~

~ 16 ~

~ 17 ~

~ 18 ~

~ 19 ~

~ 20 ~

~ 21 ~

CAT QUOTES

In his last interview before his death in 1966, sculptor Alberto Giacometti said: "If I knew that a cat was closed up behind a Rembrandt painting and was in danger of asphyxiation, I would not hesitate to destroy the canvas immediately to liberate the animal."

A lithe and agile breed.

CAT SNIPS

In the 1920s when a literary circle gathered each day at New York's Algonquin Hotel, the group, which included Robert Benchley, James Thurber, Dorothy Parker and, occasionally, F. Scott Fitzgerald and Tennessee Williams, was always joined by a permanent resident of the Algonquin, a cat named Hamlet. The Round Table is gone, and so is Hamlet, but there is still a cat living in the hotel's lobby. Her name is Matilda.

With its "big cat" appearance the Cat of Bengal is an impressive animal of surprisingly good nature.

SUPERSTITIOUS CATS

It is unlucky to hear a cat crying before setting off on a journey. The luck can be changed if one returns to find out what the cat wants.

~ 22 ~

~ 23 ~

CAT LAW

Since 1964, it has been against the law to own more than four cats in Dallas, Texas.

~ 24 ~

~ 25 ~

~ 26 ~

~ 27 ~

~ 28 ~

PRESIDENTIAL CATS

Teddy Roosevelt, born this day in 1858, enjoyed the company of a cat named Slippers while living in the White House. Slippers, who was often the center of attention at official functions, was a polydactyl, a cat with extra toes. Most cats have four toes, but some inherit the tendency to grow six or even seven

Cats always land on their feet.

A British Shorthair and kitten.

The British Shorthair has large, widely spaced eyes of arresting directness set in a handsome, round face.

CAT SNIPS

Micetto, a large blue and red tabby cat, was born in the Vatican and raised by Pope Leo XII.

~ 29 ~

~ 30 ~

CAT SNIPS

If you see a black cat silhouetted against the moon tonight, what did you expect? … It's Halloween! The ancient pagan feast of the dead, now celebrated on Allhallow's Eve, the night before the Christian feast of All Saint's Day, is the night witches and warlocks gather for wild sabbats and are sometimes seen flying from one to another on broomsticks with their feline "familiars." But not to worry. How could anyone – even a witch – who owns a cat be all bad?

~ 31 ~

CAT BREEDS

Manx

The tailless Manx is a native of the Isle of Man, an island steeped in Celtic folklore and situated midway between England and Ireland. Legend has it that invaders of the island cut off the tails of all the Manx cats to decorate their helmets. Mother cats, anxious to save their kittens from harm, bit off their tails at birth until, eventually, the kittens were born tailless. While it is also maintained that the Manx was transported from Japan to the British Isles by Phoenician traders, its most probable origin is that in 1558, a ship from the Spanish Armada was wrecked off the coast of the Isle of Man and tailless cats on board swam ashore to become the ancestors of the modern Manx.

A Manx Cat Club was formed in 1901 and England's King Edward VII was known to have several of these cats as pets. The Manx can be seen in three stages of taillessness: the "rumpy," completely without a tail, the "stumpy" and the "longie," each showing residual tails of varying lengths. The rumpy possesses a lethal factor in that kittens born of two rumpy parents are often stillborn.

The Manx cat.

The Manx has a solid, stocky frame and a distinctively rounded rump and, of course, little or no tail.

~ *November* ~

"A cat should be handled gently and kept as calm as possible during the judging. Women are naturally more gentle in their methods, and more tender-hearted. When my pets are entered in competition, may some wise, kind woman have the judging of them!"

Helen Winslow, 1900

November's cat is deeply emotional and should be treated with great care if harmony is to be established.

~ November ~

~ 1 ~

CAT STARS

Orangey, the star of Breakfast at Tiffany's and other films, was most famous for his title role in Rhubarb, opposite Ray Milland, filmed when the cat was sixteen years old. Orangey was a natural clown who would leap into the air or into a swimming pool with just a nod from his trainer, Frank Inn, and repeat the stunt as many times as the director required until the stunt looked just right for the camera. He was paid a thousand dollars a week for his work, plus, of course, a little tidbit of food for each trick and every repetition.

~ 2 ~

~ 3 ~

~ 4 ~

~ 5 ~

CAT SNIPS

Note for show cats… Siamese cats kept in high temperature conditions will produce a lighter, more desirable coat. Conversely, a drop in temperature produces a much darker coat color.

~ 6 ~

~ 7 ~

PERSONALITY CATS

Vivien Leigh
(b. November 5, 1913 –
d. July 8, 1967)
British stage and screen star, famous for her feline type of grace and beauty, Vivien Leigh won Academy Awards for her role as Scarlett O'Hara in Gone With the Wind in 1939, and as Blanche du Bois in Tennessee Williams's Streetcar Named Desire in 1951. Vivien Leigh and her husband Sir Laurence Olivier owned two seal point Siamese males, Boy and New. The cats traveled by Vivien's side whenever she went on tour. New was named for the New Theatre in London, with which she and Sir Laurence were closely connected.

A playful Seal Point Siamese kitten.

Narrow and delicate, the Siamese is an instantly recognizable breed and one of the most popular pedigrees.

SUPERSTITIOUS CATS
No cat which has been bought will ever be any good at catching mice.

~ 8 ~

~ 9 ~

CELEBRITY CATS
When the author Colette visited New York, she overheard a pair of cats having a friendly chat with one another. "Finally!," she said, "I've found someone who speaks French!"

~ 10 ~

~ 11 ~

~ 12 ~

CAT SNIPS
In the 9th century, King Henry I of Saxony decreed that the fine for killing a cat should be sixty bushels of corn.

~ 13 ~

~ 14 ~

PERSONALITY CATS

Claude Rains
*(b. November 10, 1889 –
d. May 30, 1967)*
An English-born actor of stage and screen, Claude Rains became established as a member of the Hollywood elite and played opposite Humphrey Bogart and Ingrid Bergman in Casablanca. His first major part in American movies was the title role of Caesar in Cecil B. DeMille's Caesar and Cleopatra. His co-star was the kittenish Vivien Leigh, a fitting part for an actor well-known in Hollyood as a thoroughly dedicated cat person.

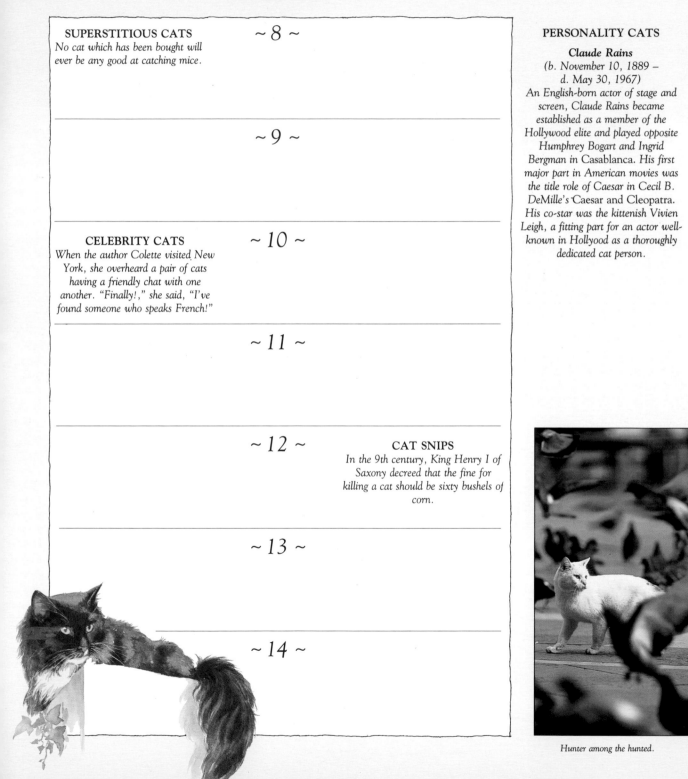

Hunter among the hunted.

The Angora is named after Ankara in Turkey, from where it originates, and makes an affectionate, playful pet.

~ November ~

~ 15 ~

~ 16 ~

CARTOON CATS

Duchess is the elegant Persian cat created for Walt Disney's 1970 animated feature, The Aristocats. In the story, she is abducted to the French countryside where she encounters a Dickensian assortment of animal characters, and elists the aid of O'Malley, the alley cat, to help her escape and find her way back home.

A classically proportioned puss.

SUPERSTITIOUS CATS

Indonesians and Malays believe that if you wash your cat, it will bring rain.

~ 17 ~

~ 18 ~

~ 19 ~

CAT FACTS

A cat's teeth, from the tiniest kitten to the biggest lion, are the most awesome weapons in the animal kingdom. They are quite sharp, of course, but are also serrated like a steak knife. The curved, pointed canines are set in the cat's jaw so that the molars fit together with their sides intact, like a pair of scissors, rather than crown to crown, as is the case in humans and most other mammals.

The pretty California Spangled Cat.

~ 20 ~

~ 21 ~

The large, appealing eyes of the California Spangled Cat are defined by fine black rims.

~ 22 ~

~ 23 ~

~ 24 ~

The nonchalantly beautiful Colorpoint.

ARTISTIC CATS

In 1968 when photographer Philipe Halsman worked for a fast-action shot that would capture the wild surrealism of artist Salvador Dali, one of his assistants tossed water at the painter and each of three others threw live cats at him. It took twenty-six attempts to get the composition exactly right, but the cats were professionally patient through it all. So, it should be added, was Dali.

~ 25 ~

WAR CATS

During the Vietnam War, the U.S. Army sent cats into the action in hopes that their fabled night vision would help guide soldiers on patrol in the jungle after dark. But, as the official report explains, the cats didn't win any medals: "A squad, on being ordered to move out, was led off in different directions by the cats; on some occasions, the cats led their troops racing through thick brush in pursuit of mice and birds. Troops had to force the cats to follow the direction of the patrol – a practice that often led to the animals stalking and attacking the dangling pack straps of soldiers marching directly in front of them. If the weather was inclement, or even threatening, the cats were never anywhere to be found."

CAT FACTS

The following extraordinary item appeared in the Japan Daily Herald *on November 26, 1877: "In order to escape cholera, the dogs in the Matsushima neighborhood, the cats and birds in Horiye, the monkeys and bears in Nambajinchi, the rabbits in the Temma Temple and the deer in Sakurnomiya Temple are wearing charms.*

~ 26 ~

~ 27 ~

SUPERSTITIOUS CATS

In Denmark, as recently as the turn of the century, it was customary to bury cats alive under one's doorstep to bring good luck to the house.

~ 28 ~

The Colorpoint, or Himalayan, makes an extremely good house cat of great charm.

~ 29 ~

CELEBRITY CATS

Born on this day in 1835, Samuel Clemens, whose pen name was Mark Twain, often wrote about cats and seldom worked without one, or several, on hand to help him. He once said that "If a man could be crossed with a cat, it would improve the man but deteriorate the cat."

~ 30 ~

PERSONALITY CATS

Sir Winston Spencer Churchill
*(b. November 30, 1874 –
d. January 24, 1965)
Winston Churchill, war correspondent, author and Prime Minister of England during the Second World War, owned a cat named Jock who attended many wartime Cabinet meetings. Rumor has it that meals in the Churchill household could not begin until the ginger-colored tabby was present at the table.*

The long-necked California Spangled Cat.

The feline will habitually find a place that's "safe" for its infamous naps. Roofs, windowsills and walls all suffice.

~ *December* ~

I like little pussy, her coat is so warm;
And if I don't hurt her, she'll do me no harm,
So I'll not pull her tail, nor drive her away,
But pussy and I very gently will play.
She shall sit by my side, and I'll give her some food;
And she'll love me because I am gentle and good.

I'll pat pretty pussy, and then she will purr;
And thus show her thanks for my kindness to her.
But I'll not pinch her ears, nor tread on her paw,
Lest I should provoke her to use her sharp claw.
I never will vex her, nor make her displeased –
For pussy don't like to be worried and teased.

Anon, c.1830

The December cat is a happy-go-lucky puss that will prove a diligent mouser and entertaining character.

~ December ~

~ 1 ~

SUPERSTITIOUS CATS
*In Western Europe it is widely
believed that if a cat washes over its
ears it is a sign of rain.*

CARTOON CATS

*Top Cat was created in 1961 for his
own television show by Hanna-
Barbera, who also gave us "The
Flintstones," "Huckleberry Hound"
and "Yogi Bear." Top Cat, an alley
cat with a street-wise personality,
was the personification of the "cool
cats" of the 1950s.*

~ 2 ~

~ 3 ~

~ 4 ~

~ 5 ~

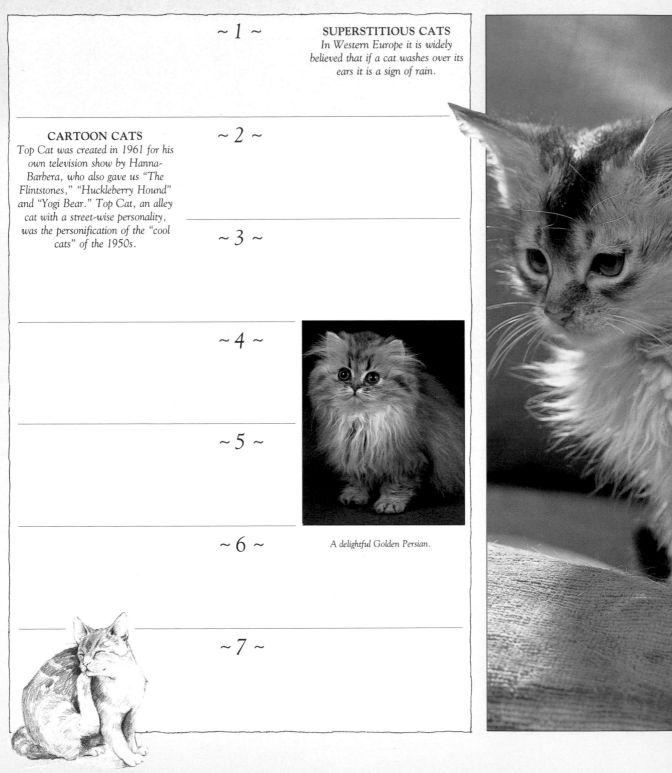

A delightful Golden Persian.

~ 6 ~

~ 7 ~

Gentle, friendly cats – Somalis make good parents as well as pets and are highly commended for their good looks.

~ December ~

CAT QUOTES
"A cat can be trusted to purr when she is pleased, which is more than can be said of human beings."

William (Dean) Inge (1860-1954)

~ 8 ~

~ 9 ~

~ 10 ~

~ 11 ~

SUPERSTITIOUS CATS
When cats rush about wildly clawing at curtains and cushions, it means that a wind is coming.

~ 12 ~

~ 13 ~

~ 14 ~

Good breeding shows in these Chinchillas.

PERSONALITY CATS

Edward G. Robinson
(b. December 12, 1893 –
d. January 26, 1973)
A Hollywood star best remembered for his portrayal of gangsters in such classics as Little Caesar and Double Indemnity, the real-life Robinson was a cultured man, a famous art collector fluent in eight languages. He was also the devoted owner of a Siamese cat, often photographed with him by the pool at his luxurious Hollywood home.

Longhaired cats who enjoy the outdoors will be time-consuming pets as their coats will get very tangled.

~ December ~

SUPERSTITIOUS CATS
When cats sit with their back to the fire, look out for frost or a storm.

~ 15 ~

~ 16 ~

~ 17 ~

CAT SNIPS
According to legend, the "M" marking on the forehead of the tabby cat was created by the Prophet Mohammed when he rested his hand on the brow of his favorite cat.

~ 18 ~

CARTOON CATS
Fritz the Cat, created by Robert Crumb for the so-called underground "Comix" in the 1960s became the subject of an animated film by Ralph Bakshi in 1972. Angered by what he called a "misuse" of his character, Crumb wrote a story in which Fritz was brutally murdered by an ostrich named Andrea and publicly removed himself ... and Fritz ... from any future projects involving the strange anti-social cat.

~ 19 ~

~ 20 ~

~ 21 ~

PERSONALITY CATS

Betty Grable
(b. December 18, 1916 –
d. July 2, 1973)
A popular actress, dancer and singer, Grable's famous legs danced their way through such 1940s films as The Diamond Horseshoe, The Dolly Sisters and Mother Wore Tights. Married and divorced from one-time child star Jackie Coogan, and bandleader Harry James, Betty Grable was devoted to cats and allowed her own to wander through her Hollywood home at will.

Tabby cat and bronze.

~ *The Cat Lover's Yearbook* ~

The European Shorthair comes in many different coat and color combinations and this dramatic silver and black tabby is most impressive.

~ December ~

~ 22 ~

~ 23 ~

CAT SNIPS
On Christmas Eve, according to the folklore of the English Cotswolds, cats can be conversed with – if addressed in rhyme.

~ 24 ~

~ 25 ~

SUPERSTITIOUS CATS
A black cat in the audience on opening night portends a successful run for a play.

~ 26 ~

~ 27 ~

~ 28 ~

Who knows what cats think of?

PERSONALITY CATS

Cleveland Amory
(b. September 2, 1917)
The author of such commentaries on social history as The Proper Bostonians *and* Who Killed Society, *Cleveland Amory, a former columnist for Saturday Review and critic for TV Guide, created what has become a perennial American classic in 1987 with* The Cat Who Came for Christmas, *the tale of his own transformation from the independence of single life in Manhattan to finding himself owned by a scruffy alley cat.*

In 1967, Amory established the Fund for Animals, located at 200 W. 57th Street in New York City, and dedicated himself, as the fund's unpaid president, to ending cruelty to animals in all forms.

His dedication for The Cat Who Came for Christmas *is:*
"To the biographee, the best cat in the whole world – with the exception, of course, of yours."

This appealing Silver Somali kitten is quite a little charmer!

~ December ~

The next Chinese Year of the Cat is 1999.

~ 29 ~

Angora & Turkish Van

The Angora cat arrived in Europe at the end of the sixteenth century, when it was first taken to France by scientist Claude Fabri de Peirese. This lovely cat originated in the Turkish city of Angora – now known as Ankara. Much admired for its long silky coat and quiet, graceful charm, the Angora's body was long and slender in what was known as the "oriental" type. An English writer in 1868 described the Angora as "a beautiful variety with silvery hair of fine texture, generally longer on the neck, but also on the tail." The white variety of the Angora was often felt to be the only true representative of the breed, and consequently Ankara Zoo established a breeding colony of whites.

~ 30 ~

CAT SNIPS

Rudyard Kipling, born this day in 1865, was the author, among many other works, of the Just So Stories, the most delightful of which is "The Cat That Walked by Himself." In it, Kipling succeeds in summing up the feline psyche:

"I am not a friend, and I am not a servant. I am the cat that walks by himself and I wish to come into your cave." But the animal also makes the point that "all places are alike to me," and makes no special promises in return for the hospitality. "I will be kind to the baby when I am in the cave" he says, "as long as he does not pull my tail too hard ... but still I am the cat who walks by himself."

~ 31 ~

The Angora is known by other names in its native homeland, usually according to color. For instance, the red tabby variety is known as the sarman; the silver tabby is the teku and the odd-eyed white is known as the Ankara kedi. Another true-breeding variety which evolved within the Angora breed is the Turkish Van. Living high in the mountainous regions of Lake Van, these cats are white with attractive auburn accents restricted to the ears and tail. Understandably perhaps, the Van is an excellent swimmer, which has earned it the name of the Swimming Cat in Turkey.

The Turkish Van, an unusual breed.

A litter of Turkish Vans before the appearance of their auburn patching.

Most unusually, *the Turkish Van enjoys playing in water and sheds a great deal of its coat in the summer.*

~ *Aquarius* ~

(January 21 – February 19)
The sign of the WATER BEARER

Tolerant, reserved, idealistic

Resembling the Capricornian cat in its dependability when the influence of Saturn is strong, the Aquarian cat becomes extrovert and rebellious when the influence of Uranus prevails. There is, therefore, an unpredictability factor to this cat which is most disconcerting. More intelligent than the average feline, this one remains unperturbed in moments of crisis, consequently making a born leader with a singular sense of vision – attributable to the third all-seeing eye which is said to be invisibly lodged in the middle of the Aquarian forehead. In Egyptian mythology this is called the Eye of Horus.

A seeker of truth (key word: I know), the Aquarian cat is a dab hand (paw) at the old "penetrating looks" ploy and meeting its cold calculating eye can be an edifying experience for its all-too-human owner. All is not such an uncomfortable ride as would at first appear, however, as the positive traits to the nature of the Aquarian cat are that it can be caring, intuitive (!), friendly, loyal and trustworthy. Often of slender build with widely spaced eyes and pointed ears, health problems are connected with the legs, teeth, general circulation and nervous system. Guard against damage to ankles, toothache and gum disease.

Compatible signs: *Libra and Gemini*

~ *Pisces* ~

(February 20 – March 20)
The sign of the FISH

Imaginative, peace-loving and kind

Pisces is the twelfth and last sign of the Zodiac. The dreamy Piscean cat is an idealist and unless constantly reminded otherwise, will exist in a fantasy world of its own making. Imaginative and warm-hearted, these delightful creatures are among life's "gentle folk," full of understanding and forgiveness and far too "nice" for this wicked world! The feline Piscean will avoid awkward situations like the plague, veering into the warm security of sunnier, trouble-free waters.

It dislikes critiscism and will refuse to admit that it was the culprit who missed the litter tray, firmly convincing itself that some other cat was the guilty party. Often in agonies of indecision, this unhappy state of affairs tends to be a problem to the Piscean puss who will procrastinate and delay the evil moment when choices simply have to be made. Notwithstanding, this little cat with its small, shapely body and luminous eyes can achieve an almost psychic relationship with its owner or, less esoterically, can be the most sympathetic and supportive of companions. Two fishes swimming in opposite directions is the traditional Piscean symbol. It is not surprising, therefore, that the Piscean cat often takes to water quite easily. Pisces rules the feet, liver and circulation. Guard against cat flu and diseases of the liver.

Compatible signs: *Cancer and Scorpio*

(March 21 – April 20)
The sign of the RAM

New beginnings, energy, leadership

Aries is the first sign of the Zodiac and the Arian cat typifies the glorious sense of awakening, rebirth and joyousness connected with the Vernal Equinox. He is courageous, volatile, assertive – and a dedicated lover! The male Arian cat is the eternal "ginger tom from next door" while the female of the species is a flighty feline temptress. Both impossible flirts, each possesses a fiery temper – understandable since Aries is a Fire sign – and the sparks will fly when the object of the male Arian's desire cries off with a headache!

Physically very active, the Arian cat shows a fine disregard for its owner's treasured ornaments which may come to grief during a sudden fit of indoor gymnastics. This is a cat of energetic demeanor and with a quick, darting appearance. Tending towards lean and wiry and with a long slender neck, the Arian cat often manifests its Fire sign associations with a red or ruddy coat color. Health problems most likely are those connected with the head, brain, upper jaw and carotid arteries. Guard against eye troubles, toothache and feverish sickness such as cat flu.

(April 21 – May 21)
The sign of the BULL

Steadfast, courageous and firm

The Taurean cat is a good old-fashioned puss cat. Flighty this one is not – preferring domestic bliss and home comforts to naughty nights out on the tiles! Too many "home comforts" however lead to a typically sturdy Taurean physique, therefore appetite should be carefully monitored to avoid obesity. More territorially minded than most, this cat fiercely defends its own back yard against all comers and the formidable Taurean frame with fur furiously "bushed" is sufficient to discourage the most determined intruder.

Solidly built with bull-like neck and powerful shoulders, the manner of the Taurean is ponderous and its gait slow and deliberate. But make no mistake, in pursuance of sensual gratification – attributable to ruling planet Venus – and having attached itself to hearth, home (and board) of its humans, this feline will be a loyal and dependable friend for life. Positive traits of the Taurean cat are those of compassion, trustworthiness and practicality. Negative traits are jealousy, possessiveness and self-indulgence. There is also a tendency to attach too much significance to conservative ideas – hence a lack of flair and imagination! Vulnerable parts of the body are the neck, throat, ears and the back of the head. Guard against throat infections and obesity.

Compatible signs: *Leo and Sagittarius.*   **Compatible signs:** *Virgo and Capricorn*

~ Gemini ~

(May 22 – June 21)
The sign of the TWINS

Duality, versatility, the intellect

Exuberant and energetic, the Geminian cat is the quintessential "playful pussy" with a mental dexterity which makes this cat the ideal companion for a like-minded human. Versatile and adaptable, this busy little feline is a great conversationalist and its vivacious chirping could well charm birds, traditionally associated with this sign, out of trees! Graceful in build with quick, darting eyes, the Gemininian cat is constantly active with a nervous energy springing from a seemingly endless source. Not surprising that Mercury, quicksilver messenger of the gods, is Gemini's ruling planet.

Gracious and charming but preferring to orchestrate relationships on its own terms, the Gemini cat is not a "cuddly" little creature and can sometimes be a puzzling, enigmatic soul reflecting the duality of its birth sign. A love of open spaces and fresh air also echoes the Mutable-Air sign of the planet Gemini. The chatty little Gemini cat, however, can cause complete chaos with its restless romping around the home. Plants are ravaged, curtains climbed, knick-knacks knocked over and whose are those claw marks on the coffee table? Though usually making a swift recovery from most illnesses, health problems are experienced with the legs, shoulders and lungs.

Compatible signs: *Libra and Aquarius*

~ Cancer ~

(June 22 – July 23)
The sign of the CRAB

Sensitive, maternal and very romantic

The Cancerian cat makes for a highly domesticated and dedicated home-loving feline – if female, the perfect Mom Cat. Unless destined to become a breeding queen or the male, a stud cat, the responsible owner is recommended to consider spaying or neutering, since nothing short of this will convince the Cancerian cat that it was not born to proliferate. Neutering, however, will not diminish this cat's kindly concern for all small furries. On the contrary, its strong maternal instinct will extend to other family pets who could find themselves borne off to the warm, comfortable nest of the Cancerian cat. For these concerned caring folk are the feline equivalent of the human "lovely person."

Ruled by the Moon and therefore often over-sensitive and vulnerable to the negative effects of disharmony, they are generally plump and cuddly with kind, sweet expressions set in round, moon-like faces. Cancer rules the stomach, so that these cats are prone to digestive upsets – particularly during times of stress. Guard against stomach ulcers, problems with the female reproductive organs and illnesses which require special diets.

Compatible signs: *Pisces and Scorpio*

~ *Leo* ~

(July 24 – August 23)
The sign of the LION

Self-confidence, enthusiasm, pride

Flamboyant, big-hearted and with a strong sense of dignity, the leonine Leo cat can certainly equate with the title "The King of Cats." Demanding lots and lots of attention – and generally getting it – these fulsome Leo traits can often become negative to produce a vain, arrogant and domineering cat. While traditionally Leo cats sport luxuriant coats of red or gold, not all of these splendid creatures possess the brilliant colors of their ruling planet the Sun. Coat condition of most Leo cats, however, is often quite spectacular.

These felines usually make excellent parents – the male a proud, protective father and the female, a wise and caring mother. Leo will always repay the love and attention received from its adoring owner (subject) with generosity, loyalty and a rare companionship until the end of its days. The bearing of the Leo cat is bold, regal and fearless. Its eyes are large, bright and impress all with their authoritative gaze. Leo cats are prone to heart and circulatory problems with a possiblity of anemia. Guard against diseases of the spine.

~ *Virgo* ~

(August 24 – September 23)
The sign of the VIRGIN

Discriminative, methodical, logical

The cat, thought of as a feminine animal, is usually associated with the astrological sign of Virgo. Certainly, this fastidiously clean, intelligent puss, often applying a fine sense of logic to achieve its own ends – plus lashings of laid-back charm – sums up most succinctly the Virgoan character. Compulsive coat and whisker washers, the Virgoan cat is an independent character who appreciates delicately prepared and regular meals.

A real cool cat who is not particularly demonstrative, this puss likes his or her own space and often exhibits a painstaking fastidiousness regarding its health and hygiene. This can pave the way to a downright "finicky" cat. If this does occur, tempt the fussy feeder with small, frequent and tasty meals. If mealtimes are still angst-ridden, make sure that the small, frequent and tasty meals also involve deliciously inviting aromas. The independent character of this agreeable cat, plus a subdued sense of adventure, make the Virgoan feline a good choice for the career person. Parts of the Virgoan puss most prone to infection are the bowels, intestines and abdomen. Guard against diarrhea and treat regularly for worms.

Compatible signs: *Aries and Sagittarius*   **Compatible signs:** *Capricorn and Taurus*

~ Libra ~

~ Scorpio ~

Libra

(September 24 – October 23)
The sign of the SCALES

Balance, justice, love of beauty

A lover of harmony and peace, the Libran cat is intelligent, charming and makes a fine, sensitive companion – turning in beautifully to its owner's every mood. Venus, goddess of love and beauty, is the ruling planet of Libra and accordingly exerts a somewhat sybaritic influence over this cat. Which can be observed in its appreciation of soft, melodious music and certain creature comforts – like the warmth and softness of its owner's bed!

A compulsive craver of comfort with just a touch of winsome appeal and "cuddliness" makes these cats ideal companions for the lonely. However, a well-balanced, sensitive soul such as this, oft given to contemplation of its clean little paws, the universe and everything, may occasionally allow itself to descend into bouts of negative thinking – despondency often alternating with fits of excitable elation, tipping the Libran's normally well-adjusted mental balance. Generally of slender and graceful proportions, the Libran cat is prone to kidney diseases, diabetic conditions and skin complaints, such as eczema, and others of an eruptive nature. Guard against skin complaints by insuring that diet is not at fault.

Scorpio

(October 24 – November 22)
The sign of the SCORPION

Tenacious, secretive, intensely psychic

The Scorpio cat has boundless energy, great strength of purpose and its actions are often motivated by the depth of its passions. Being of an intensely emotional nature, this aspect of the Scorpio cat's character, if denied, can result in a creature of almost satanic intensity. Secretive and with piercing eyes that seem to seek out their owner's innermost fears, the Scorpio cat is the feline most likely to have been the "familiar" of witches in medieval times.

Great manipulators, cats born under this sign appear to have everything under control – including their bemused owners (beware not to fall entirely under the spell of this cat!) Heavy, muscular and strong-boned, Scorpio cats are fiendishly adaptable and by some strange alchemy manage to exist on their own terms in most situations with very little trouble at all. Radiating a strong personal magnetism, cats born under this sign are both cautious yet courageous. But on the distaff side, the negative Scorpio feline is jealous, vindictive and some might think a likely candidate for re-homing! Scorpio rules the genital organs, the bladder and the colon. Guard against ulcers and hernias.

Compatible signs: *Aquarius and Gemini*

Compatible signs: *Cancer and Pisces*

~ Sagittarius ~

(November 23 – December 21)
The sign of the ARCHER

Extrovert, optimistic, independent

Sporty and with a well-developed sense of adventure, the Sagittarian cat is a happy-go-lucky feline surviving often "more by good luck than by good management." This cat's abundant energy coupled with its mis-guided missile approach to life make it a highly lovable character. The light-hearted, travel-happy attitude of the Sagittarian puss brings to mind Top Cat, the cartoon alley cat with a talent for getting into – and out of – numerous scrapes and still ending up with a smile on his face!

Given the opportunity, the Sagittarian cat is an excellent mouser and should its territory prove to be a mouse-free zone, its attention will turn to other quarries. Old potatochip bags, socks, small toys – all these trophies and more are carried back home as loving gifts for the delight (!) of its human. Of athletic build with large, expressive eyes, the adventurous Sagittarian puss loves to be the center of attention and because of its active lifestyle is more prone to accidents than most. Rheumatism – shades of those cold, damp nights on the tiles – is also a common complaint with this group. Guard aginst these problems by calling a curfew. Cosy nights by the fireside may convince this traveling cat that home is best.

Compatible signs: *Aries and Leo*

~ Capricorn ~

(December 22 – January 20)
The sign of the GOAT

Industrious, meticulous, persevering

Quiet and self-disciplined with an air of solidity and staidness gives the Capricornian cat a maturity beyond its years. Even Capricornian kittens are solemn little creatures, lacking the skittishness of their peers in other astrological groups. The Capricornian association with Father Time and and old age is the key. Averse to change, this cat is also very cautious, preferring the security of its own territory indoors to the insecurity of the great outdoors. Said to be ruled by Saturn, the Great Taskmaster of the Zodiac, the Capricornian cat is living proof that you can put old heads on young shoulders!

The element Earth, with its traditional association with caves, is strong in the Capricornian make-up accounting for the somewhat restrained attitude of this cat. For, while the Capricorn cat makes a loyal and steadfast companion, it does not bestow its affections lightly. Long-bodied and with a straight nose in an angular face, problems afflicting this sign are rheumatism, cramps and a tendency to the dislocation of bones. Skin complaints such as eczema are common. Guard against these with careful dietary planning. Also guard against toothache.

Compatible signs: *Taurus and Virgo*